CW01456903

Managing Teachers in FE

What should you put in to get the best out?

The companion volume to
Teaching in FE (ISBN 9781482730876)

You don't need to be very bright to see what's wrong.
And it's pretty simple to come up with wise suggestions.
But to find a real solution - that's another matter.

Alexander Zinoviev, *The Yawning Heights*

ISBN: 9781482730807
© Paul Eustice 2013 All rights reserved.
www.justfiedtext.co.uk
www.bpfe.org.uk

Contents

Intro - What this book is for and why is it necessary? A note on terminology and context. Up-to-date sources and resources.

1) What is FE? What is a manager? The clients for FE and managing a network

encompassing the sector – need for focus – the unique nature of FE as a business – contradictory contexts – managers and decisions – administering, managing and leading – transactional, transformational and distributed – post-heroic leaders – being better at what? – clients for FE – networks and boundary spanners.

2) Motivation and Training – how CPD becomes quality management

getting things done through other people – the language of management and taking managers seriously – motivations for managers - choice of metaphor – trust and control - appraisal – career cycle stages – what kind of CPD? – transferring good practice – stress – benefits of the group

3) Paperwork and Reality – using information to get results.

data and dissociation – fads and scepticism – evidence based decisions – using research

4) Managing time, behaviour and stress

busyness and courage – owning the problem – selecting solutions – implementing – timely action – disciplinary codes – listening – controlling meetings – negotiating – checking and evaluating - final note on stress

5) Curriculum design and managing money – their proper relationship

the main task? – funding and integrity of purpose – reduced contribution from the state – social and economic functions – enhancing curricula to model excellence - principles for design

6) Equal Opportunities – what are the real issues?

the spirit and the and letter of the law - managing and leading – key terms - clarifying the issue – protected characteristics – socio-economic factors

7) Employers and employability

what kind of a problem? - levels and strands – who is dissatisfied with whom? – work and job readiness – demand-led, but whose demands? – shortages, gaps and definitions – internal cooperation – funding engagement – engaging with whom? – importing expertise – agencies and brokers – HE and FE

Annexe 1 checklist on management speak

Annexe 2 the 'simple' rules

Bibliography

Introduction, but don't skip this bit – read it first

> Relative to the numbers employed in each occupation, managers are among the least likely to receive training (49 per cent), similar to the level found among machine operatives and elementary and administrative staff.
> *National Employer Skills Survey for England (UKCES 2009)*

What this book for and why is it necessary?

This is a text for managers. The level of responsibility and the size of organisation are irrelevant. You may be an experienced manager looking for new ways to deal with a changing sector or new responsibilities. You may be quite to the role and wondering how to get to grips with the whole complex business. In either case, you want to do the best you can and presumably approached this text hoping it might help. This is how it works.

Your time is limited so it has to be clear what a busy manager is supposed to do with new information. On the other hand, you can sometimes get better results by spending a few moments looking at the problem from a different perspective. Quick results are not the same as hasty action and little progress is made by walking quickly in the wrong direction. So what kind of balance do you need between data and reflection, information and ideas, facts and principles?

It is very easy to be overburdened with excessive information, most of which is never properly digested. If too many links or sources are provided here you could be worse off than before, downloading files with good intentions then not having time to read them, just creating a filing job and a guilty conscience without actually learning anything directly relevant to your situation. Also, as soon as the ink is dry on the paper, or the Kindle downloaded, at least one of the web sites or agencies will probably be abolished or merged as funding dries up. On the other hand, there are some very useful and information sources which, used wisely, can help you make evidence-based decisions and to plan ahead. I shall mention a few in passing, but most of the original links and footnotes have been removed from the main text which, as a result, is now much shorter, like your lunch break. Instead, if you go to www.bpfe.org.uk/links you can select from a wide range of live links which will always be up to date. That includes sources of data, policy documents, examples of good practice and newsletters. Take what you need.

The first edition was released in 2006, as an e-book entitled *Making the Difference as a Manager in FE*. Although 2006 may sound quite recent, it is still one year before the first ever Kindle was used by the public. Change is increasingly rapid and that will be one of your problems. Small changes can have widespread and unexpected effects. It is hard to keep up, let alone judge wisely which new ideas or publications are worthy of your limited time and attention. It is already quite rare to meet someone who hasn't used Kindle, so this new edition had to be formatted for use I-phones as well.

A great deal has changed in that time. In 2006 the Learning and Skills Council (LSC) had been established for five years and seemed omnipotent. Now it is already forgotten, just a collection of old policy documents and a few score people enjoying early retirement. The Dept. for Children, Schools and families only lasted three years, Connexions centres were restructured, FE funding was taken over by the Education Funding Agency (EFA) which at first referred to the Skills Funding Agency (SFA) and the Young Peoples Learning Agency (YPLA) until the YPLA disappeared. The Learning and Skills Improvement Service (LSIS) took over the Centre for Excellence in Leadership (CEL) and the Quality Improvement Agency (QIA) but even as I write this paragraph it has announced a loss of funding so, by the time the ink on this page is dry, who knows? We all learned how to spell baccalaureate (again) until we had to forget about it (again). The Institute for Learning (IFL) was established in 2002 but by 2013 was on 'transitional funding' as a new Guild was mooted. Does anyone remember the Adult Learning Inspectorate

(ALI)? What will this alphabet soup look like in another six or seven years? It is quite probable that all those Big Beasts in the jungle will have changed again, as new governments sweep away all those vital 'overarching' priorities and previously fundamental principles. Put not your trust in princes. Although, on the other hand, your need to know your way around the jungle, because that is part of your job.

There are, of course, no easy answers or magic recipes. Annexe 1 leaves you with a few simple rules, but they will make more sense after you read the book. Nor would success or failure look identical in all cases. We are all different personalities in very different local contexts, so we find our own unique way of doing what is best in that situation with those people at that time. But here are the obvious questions:

> Are there fundamental principles of management that remain valid in all contexts, however much the context may change?

> Are those principles any different for educators, as opposed to other commercial or industrial contexts?

> Are there certain key principles particular to education that remain constant in each new economic and political context?

> Should changing economic and political contexts change the way you manage?

In short, the answers are yes, yes, yes and no. You might need to add a 'but' to the last answer.

A note on terminology and context

The language we use is always important. It conveys values and sends messages of which we may be unaware.

The Life Long Learning Sector consists of several interconnected areas, only one of which is called Further Education, and not all the organisations through which FE is delivered are colleges. Increasingly, provision has been located with other 'providers', either commercial or voluntary sector, and often in partnership. Working across institutional boundaries is an important element of management and dealt with in Chapter One. There may be elements of management that are peculiar to larger institutions, with more complex bureaucracies, or to organisations that use mainly volunteer labour, and they will also be considered, but the general principles of managing people within an educational context apply all providers, including both 'adult and community' provision and organisations who used to be purely commercial but developed into educational provision recently.

What do we call those people who are using the FE system? There was a brief trend to use the term 'customers' when FE was trying to impress upon itself the idea that it was working under market forces and had to be more responsive to those it served. It was used in that sense and for that purpose by the QIA in its first consultation document (*Pursuing Excellence,* 2006). But they can't be customers, because the customer is always right and can take their trade elsewhere. Neither is true of most applicants for FE, certainly for full-time courses. The term might have been a useful corrective, reminding us that customers have to be nurtured, but it also contains the idea of customers as people to whom we sell products or services, which implies that a key function for management is to develop a saleable product and a good marketing strategy. That is only part of the picture.

'Learners' was popularised by the LSC but has never caught on with the people it refers to. It also begs a question, as not all of those enrolled are actually learning. 'Student' is more traditional and that is what most of them call themselves, so that is what they are called in this text, whatever their age or background, although it is probably not what your institution calls them at the moment.

Most FE college staff used to refer to themselves as

lecturers, and this term is still current in most formal agreements. It used to indicate status. Then teachers in schools started to earn more than FE staff. Status on inferior income is an odd concept. Also, the emphasis is very much on how we teach, which means avoiding the formal lecture in most cases. A valuable contribution to learning is also made by Learning Support Assistants, advisers and other support and administrative staff – all part of the community of learning. In a private company the term 'trainer' may be more familiar. Some readers might wish to argue about the difference between education and training, ascribing a superior form of process to 'education'. Others accept the term 'trainer' as having connotations of efficiency and value for money. For the purposes of this text it really doesn't matter. What counts is to know what students want, to make sure it is also what they need and then make sure they get it.

And that's enough prologue, so let's get on with it.

Chapter 1

What is FE and what is a manager?

The clients for FE and managing a network.

What is FE, and what is a manager?

> Further Education is pivotal to the Government's aim
> of bringing social justice and economic prosperity to
> everyone.   Sir Geoffrey Holland, Chair QIA,
> *Announcing the launch of the Excellence Gateway, June 2006*

> In order for the Council to discharge its remit it has to
> engineer cultural and relationship change through the
> development, at national and local levels, of genuine
> partnership working.   Sir George Sweeney,
> *Trust in the Future (LSC 2002)*

The fact that neither of the bodies mentioned above is still
with us does not, in itself, invalidate their statements, although
it does make the LSC's title rather ironic. FE has always been
about social justice and partnerships are fundamental to its
future. But FE has also always been abused, and we may also
note that

> It is the very diversity of FE that can present challenges
> to the professional identity of its teaching staff.
> Lingfield (2012) 4.3

Let's keep this simple for now – there will be footnotes later
for anyone who needs more detail and original sources. In 1993
colleges of FE were incorporated. Freed from the control of
local authorities, they could make their own decisions and, if
they got it wrong, go bankrupt. At roughly the same time, a

New Model Army of reformers started trampling all over the sector, using as their bible appalling statistics about high failure rates and exhorting us all to excellence, along with a great deal more paperwork to show we were pure of heart and always striving for it. Most senior managers were ex-lecturers with no experience of running business and no training in managing change. Not surprisingly, a proportion of them reacted to this new pressure by passing it on through the system. Too often, government bullied colleges who bullied their staff and there was a defensive overuse of the term 'compliance'.

In the early days, when many of the staff couldn't understand the need for radical change, it was far too easy to push rather than persuade, to mistake measurement for analysis and the reporting of data for responsibility. A zealous regime encouraged a style of management that was unsuitable for an educational system, as it relied upon and encouraged what can only be called uneducated behaviour, the kind that ignored everything we had learned about fostering change from years of research. As a result, the 'post-16' sector was expected to supply the economy with the right number of employees, trained to the right degree in whatever skills were needed in a given year and location, while its college-based managers were expected to motivate a workforce who were consistently denigrated, with their workload and bureaucracy increased, whilst real earnings declined relative to school-based colleagues.

It is particularly ironic that the rhetoric of national policy became increasingly strident about colleges being independent and showing initiative and leadership as a generation of managers were being trained to bark when and how ordered by overweening external agencies. In a related problem, external agencies that didn't trust teachers started making their own materials for them and laying down comprehensive guidelines whilst also expecting them not only to display initiative but to somehow encourage entrepreneurial skills.[1]

---

[1] discussed in more detail in *Teaching in FE* but note in particular Ecclestone (2002) and see below

Fortunately, what was most valuable in FE - the sheer arsiness of its staff - managed to withstand the experience. Lessons were learned and we entered the 21st century with a more subtle, responsive, intelligent style that may foster the growth of a well-organised, coherent community of learning. Margaret and David Collinson (Collinson 2006) point out that "colleges are important local employers and also typically confer status and credibility on the towns and cities in which they exist and operate." As enrolments increase, FE has an impact on "the lives and families of ever-larger sections of their local communities" and thus "can play a major role" which is "sometimes life changing, frequently life enhancing". This potential is a major motivator for college employees.

> While we had expected to encounter a demoralised, passive workforce, we have repeatedly interviewed staff at all hierarchical levels who are committed to their students, their colleges, the sector and the community they serve. Research interviewees have consistently talked about the importance of 'making a difference' and of enhancing the learning and social benefits for students in the UK post-16 sector.
>
> Collinson (2006) p24

I have admired the FE experience in tower blocks and 'temporary' huts that never get replaced; in prisons, hospitals and garages; in universities and a room above a cafe; in salons, theatres, recording studios and building sites, massage rooms, libraries and kitchens; in prestigious rooms rented from London clubs and societies and in old schools with original fireplaces and Victorian graffiti on the desk; in gardens, in purpose-built space-age extensions and the back of an old converted lorry. Such was the range of people benefiting from all those learning opportunities that you realise after a while that if you hadn't worked in FE you would never have known how many sub-cultures existed, how varied are the needs of an individual trying to improve their lot, to increase their understanding and abilities. All those individual journeys – inwards, upward and outwards – are what make FE worth the aggravation, and provide satisfaction for the workforce. But, in the midst of such variety, with so many people involved in so many ways to feed our economy, enrich our culture and develop the potential of our population, can we actually say clearly – what is FE? We need to step back briefly to understand the present and therefore the future.

When it was financed by the Further Education Funding Council (1992-2001) it was relatively easy to speak of an FE sector, with its special nature, purposes and client base or beneficiaries. It was, even then, a diverse and complex market. The familiar technical colleges had served local business by taking on apprentices in traditional industries. Then the economy changed and a different kind of workforce was required. FE was seen as important to the development of a more flexible, literate, skilled workforce and, partly because of its growing importance, it was also seen as requiring reform to be more efficient and effective.[2] Colleges sought new markets in new industries, but also in new functions in new sectors of the population. FE grew to include a wider range of different beneficiaries, with different needs, until the focus of activity for FE managers became so diverse that the Adult Learning Inspectorate (ALI) published their *Annual Report of the Chief Inspector 2003-4* to confirm a widely held view that

> … further education institutions are buffeted by change. They are often very big, very diverse and subject to frequent demands for limitless responsiveness. Grade profiles show that, almost certainly, that degree of responsiveness cannot be reconciled with consistently good provision. Even in the best managed colleges, there will always be areas of learning which have been newly introduced, or are

---

[2] More details of the history of FE in this respect are in the companion volume *Teaching in FE* and in a very approachable academic analysis in Lucas 2004(a).

overburdened with student demand, or are in the process of transition to meet changing circumstances of one kind or another in the wider world. (p27)

as a result of which

...very few colleges can sustain generally high standards for long. Only 45 of the 125 colleges (about 36%) that inspectors judged to be consistently good between 1993 and 1997 have stayed so since. Twenty five of those were sixth form colleges. It may well be time to review the form of governance of incorporated colleges and their relationship to government. (p28)

The figures in Oftsed's report for the Learning and Skills Sector 21011/12, using the new four point scale and expressed as a percentage, looked like this:

Context and total number of providers	Outstanding	Good	Satisfactory	Inadequate
General FE or tertiary college (45)	4	31	49	16
Sixth form college (13)	0	38	31	31
Independent specialist college (12)	17	33	33	17
Independent learning providers (128)	7	48	34	10
Adult and Community (Learning providers (63)	5	59	32	5

In trying to meet the needs of so many markets, FE as a

whole was failing to meet so many of them that it seemed private enterprise might have to step in and show them how to focus properly. This was especially so for work based programmes, and the report for 2004-5 considered that "private providers do better" because of their "greater proximity to employers". Private enterprise is "closer in structure and ethos to the companies it serves" (p13)

The call for a clear focus comes at a time when the very notion of an 'FE' sector has given way to the 'Learning and Skills' sector, starting at 14 instead of 16, and there is so little work available for our young citizens we are increasingly training them in 'entrepreneurial skills' in the hope they can grow up to invent new sources of employment for each other. Our desire to make FE not only a business in itself but clearly subservient to business in general comes at a time when 'business' in the form of banks and large companies seems to have failed our social needs. So what have we ended up with?

Within a single market, we now find general and specialist FE colleges; sixth form colleges with an increasing percentage of vocational work; schools with sixth forms forming consortia to offer vocational options; academies, adult education institutions under various forms of funding; private and voluntary sector providers. They form various combinations and many of them are selecting from the wide range of potential clients a small number or a narrowly defined group to whom they can offer a particularly efficient service.

The White Paper *Raising Skills, Improving Life Chances* (DfES 2006) made it very clear that colleges will be subject to a sustained effort to sharpen up their act by providing them with expertise from industry and with more competition (5.29, 7.3, forward 32). Offering "more choice" to employers and students means encouraging colleges to

> Focus more on providing a skilled workforce, which may mean giving up the social mission involved in adult ed and allow the voluntary sector to take it over (2.48, forward 20)

Specialise in certain vocational sectors (2.11)

Consider consortia with other organisations, which might include other providers but also forming "not-for-profit charities with other organisations, including businesses, schools, community groups and universities" (5.26, forward 31).

National performance figures show that specialisation does not in itself increase quality. This may be partly because specialisation is inflicted most often on schools and colleges that are already failing, a cure used only *in extremis,* but certainly the idea that being specialised will in itself increase quality is flawed. It might facilitate better focus which then brings quality, but that is a different argument.

Private trainers may offer NVQs in a given vocational specialism and remove business from the local college. They may work with schools to offer vocational options, which used to be a college speciality. At the other extreme, colleges other were permitted to buy up local schools, forming academies in their area as part of a major expansion[3]. "What is FE?" becomes better phrased as "what would your institution be advised to become if it wants to survive?" FE covers such a range of potential beneficiaries, it is a business decision as to which of them you should consider to be your market.

Or rather, it would be, if FE were a business like any other. But it isn't.

---

[3] The main business of the VT Group is military supplies to the British and UK governments, but by 2006 it had bought up Touchstone Learning and Skills, a work-based learning provider, at a cost of £12m, bringing its annual income from education to a figure of £100m. Manchester College of Art and Technology (Mancat) and Barnfield in Luton, for example, were given permission to sponsor academies, at £2m per academy and this trend continues. The relationship of colleges to local schools had changed from servants of capricious customers to potential owners/governors/sponsors.

While performance can be measured in the private sector on a common basis, a clear measure of performance such as profit is absent from the public sector. Further, given the nature and 'social role' of public services, the performance indicators employed needed to be rather different to those of the private sector and so the application of private sector measures is problematic.

Smith and Bailey (2006) p4

A college's major funding source is, for the moment, likely to remain whatever government agency is in force this year. Their formal function is that of the largest customer, although their dominance is such that most colleges behave as if the college belonged to them – a distinction that will matter more in due course. They follow government priorities in a local context. A local general college of FE (GFE) may therefore find itself under pressure to provide services for certain groups that national government or local agencies consider in need but which private enterprise would not accept.

If there are local adolescents not in education, employment and training (NEET) then the college may be asked to undertake a contract to help them, like the old, poorly funded Entry to Employment (E2E). In some cases, colleges will argue that the contract is uneconomic and it will go instead to a local voluntary agency, like NACRO, who have lower overheads, or the Prince's Trust. Some colleagues will heave a sigh of relief that such difficult clients are no longer their problem, but another college may decide that fees for certain disadvantaged groups ought to be subsidised from the overall budget, because an economic fee would be beyond such individuals, and they ought not to be disbarred by pricing mechanism from any access to their local educational facility. So is it a manager's job in FE to maximise profits, to select the most profitable markets, to obtain funding to serve the community or to serve the community within the budgets provided? What, exactly, is a manager *for* in this context?

To many people, this is a deeply personal question. They entered education for a reason, and their motivation may have been tied to notions of social purpose. Most will have started as teachers, often motivated by a self-image that included ideas about service to the community, of being useful and helping others to develop, helping the less able to flourish whilst developing the gifted and talented regardless of socio-economic background. To cast aside those who cannot afford the new service, or abandon a sector of the community because they no longer make business sense, is deeply troubling to them. On the other hand, it is hard to deny that, historically, when FE tries to help the widest possible market, it fails many of them badly. It has been subject to so many reforms partly because it has such poor retention and achievement rates. That means it has allowed thousands of people to enrol hopefully, then later to drop out or fail. In asking "whom should we help?" inspectors would no doubt argue that we also have to ask "whom are we capable of helping properly?"

Actions intended to be helpful may not be. Managers operate in a context of government policy, which is often confused and contradictory.

Pressures to improve teaching and learning in FE are driven by concerns other than the nature of teaching and learning. Over the last 50 years, there have been repeated calls for the improvement of teaching and learning in FE in attempts to tackle broader issues including perceived social and moral problems among youth, the inadequacy of vocational education and training from the point of view of employers, insufficient skill levels to ensure the nation's global competitiveness, and the need for a cost-effective FE service. Beneath these calls for improvement lies a basic problem that bedevils FE – the demand that the sector provide effective responses to some of the country's major social, employment and economic needs, and with ever-decreasing resources.

Statsz and Wright (2004), speaking particularly of the vocational field, claimed that:

> Current policy ... tends to conflate purposes and therefore lump all perceived problems together. Thus, one sees vocational learning programmes that aim to widen participation, improve the general attainment of qualifications and skills by young people and rectify skills gaps.... this conflation of economic and social purposes.... creates a situation where relatively more disadvantaged young people become the pool of candidates who are expected to add to the proportion of individuals with level 3 qualifications (4.4)

> Moreover, it is not clear what policy to expand options for 14-16 year olds wants to achieve. It could create a mass system of vocational and work-based learning for the 40% of the age group who do not achieve five 'good' GCSEs. Or it could create a more marginal system. Will 10% or 90% of this group take this route?
> (5.2)

This confusion has not been clarified yet. It is one thing to help schools motivate their less committed students by offering vocational link courses, basing the options on what will appeal to them. It is quite another to meet local market needs by analysing how many hairdressers the economy actually needs, and a third thing altogether to raise achievement levels overall, partly by more careful selection at entry.

So any decisions made by a local manager will have to allow for the possibility that all the options for which he or she can obtain funding and legal permission will be mired in confusion and contradiction. In any case, how much of management has anything to do with decision making?

Taking decisions or just taking the blame?

Handy (1985) pointed out long ago that a group of managers, asked to record the decisions they made over a week, might be hard pressed to remember any (p361). A typically simple view of college hierarchies would imply that there are different levels of 'management' - senior managers take strategic decisions, themselves constrained by external policies, whilst middle managers are tasked to apply both internal and external policies under collective responsibility. The policies may be dysfunctional, but it is their job to make staff comply with them. Lower still in the hierarchy are teachers, often said to be 'managing' a small team or even 'managing' learning in the classroom. 'Managing' becomes a term for responsibility with greater or lesser degrees of freedom to make any real decisions about that for which you are responsible.

Handy also reminds us that there will always be limits to what can be altered in the short term. The wider context includes not just formal goals set elsewhere but organisational cultures. The immediate context includes structures and individuals that cannot simply be replaced overnight. But they can, at least, be properly understood, the situation 'diagnosed' accurately to avoid unsuitable responses:

> Too many times ... low morale is met by exhortation or a Christmas party, poor communication by briefing meetings or a house journal. (p 366)

Not that all managers necessarily welcome the ability to make changes, or even to face up to them:

> Change is to managers what motherhood is to men, 'something to be approved of but for someone else. (p371)

And one always has to accept, he argues, that "compromise

has its own morality" (ibid 372). However, it is not insignificant that Handy himself actually left his job as an oil executive because he so disliked "the organisational life, the corporate life. I like to do things my own way".[4] He also claims, however figuratively, that he "fell asleep in my own lectures". That does not invalidate his comments on managing or their relevance to education, but it is always worth underlining that it is easier to advise from outside than to remain in post and somehow cope with these organisational pressures, to think independently within the system and to maintain standards under pressure. It is a cliché used in many industries that those with the get- up-and-go tend to do precisely that. The challenge is to keep the energetic critics inside, still contributing. Or, as President Lyndon Johnson once put it, inside the tent pissing out.

In brief, it is often naive to think of managers who spend their working life taking decisions and changing things as a result. But if all they do is take responsibility for what would happen anyway, are they worth the salary?

Managing, administering or leading?

Incorporation was a defining moment which tested the mettle of FE managers and, in many institutions, created a dysfunctional culture from which we are still recovering.[5] Many managers were ex-teachers, promoted through the ranks with no serious training for the new role. Suddenly, they were responsible for a multi-million pound independent business which, if it failed, would be left unprotected from financial ruin and closure. The major source of income came from LSC contracts, with stringent conditions attached. At the same time, inspections became increasingly searching and complex with shifting goalposts and decreasing wriggle room.

This led to an increased need for accurate data, not only for

---

[4] Interview, Independent careers column 27th April 2006.
[5] The legacy of 'macho management' and the relationship between management theory, gender and equal opportunities will be discussed more fully, under 'motivation' in chapter 2 and equal opportunities in chapter 6.

the new paymasters and inspectors but to inform decisions with serious consequences. Data was often unavailable or, more often, unreliable, because systems were slack and staff did not take the problem seriously. To most employees who were not managers, and were not directly aware of the logic behind it, a sudden increase in bureaucracy, allied to an increase in teaching hours, was just an annoyance. If managers insisted, sometimes in shrill and nervous tones, on the primacy of formal enrolments and register marking, it could sound just petty, so they responded unenthusiastically, or with passive resistance. The increased insistence on compliance pitted managers who sounded to staff as if they were petty and self-serving against staff who sounded to managers irresponsible and uncooperative.

Seeking to adapt to the new criteria, and under pressure, some managers were seduced by a clichéd, excessively macho view of managerial behaviour inherited from the worst examples of the commercial and industrial sector. This led them to focus on targets and tasks, not on the people who worked for them and actually comprised the organisation, those whose skills and effort were required to create the learning which was, in fact, the prime purpose of the organisation. They confused compliance with reform, and superficial control systems with management.

Having poisoned the wells, central government then asked rather petulantly why managers in FE were not managing better, and expected them to become 'leaders'. Calls were made for an improvement to management (Clark 2004, Lumby et al 2005) but the education necessary to achieve it, as so often happens, was offered long after the moment when it was first needed – prior to incorporation. Incidentally, it is not only management within FE that has been subject to calls for reform. The Council for Excellence in Management and Leadership published a report in 2002 concluding that, for business in general

a national strategy should be implemented to improve

business leaders' understanding of the importance of management and leadership development to business performance, and to ensure that the supply side responds effectively to those business imperatives.

CEML (2002) paras 41-43

Part of the training they had investigated was provided within FE, which they describe as the second most important provider, handling, for example, 42% of training for the steel industry. So FE needs not only to manage itself better, but to teach others how to manage at the same time. Most colleges, after all, have Business and Management departments. How much influence do their experts on management have on the management of the college, or is teaching the subject unrelated to actually doing it in the organisational mind set? And how well-managed are such departments? The CEL suggested we should train students elected as course or union reps and perhaps even certificate them as leaders of the future[6].

In the terminology of the 21st Century, it is now common to speak not of the difference between good and bad management but of the difference between management and leadership. The modern terminology assumes that 'managers' try to control people, and can spend a lot of time insisting on a set of largely ignored rules and procedures, whereas 'leaders' encourage a culture of self-control, so that appropriate values and habits are internalised. The National College for School Leadership (NCSL), for example, claim that managers are given a position then seek to control and organise through systems and structures to bring about efficiency. They administer the present. Leaders take the initiative and take risks to inspire others to share their goals and values, so they can bring about effectiveness. They focus on people and form the future. (NCSL 2006)

There are assumptions built in to the rhetoric of 'leadership', and indeed into the idea of associated 'training',

[6] FE Focus (TES) 4th August 2006

that need to be questioned, but there are also important principles at stake about how individuals can most usefully relate to each other in organisations, and how much energy any manager ought to spend in trying too obviously to control others.

> Too much control is expensive, time-consuming and self-defeating in motivational terms (Handy 375)

Herding cats is an unprofitable pastime, and nobody wants to employ sheep.

At institutional level, that was admitted by the LSC, who announced in their circular about plan-led funding (0309 June 2003) that:

> New planning, funding and accountability arrangements, based on greater partnership and trust are at the core of the new framework for quality and success.

And if those principles work between institutions, they also apply to individuals within the institution.

Another set of commonly made distinctions is between

> transactional leadership (or management)
> transformational leadership
> distributed or shared transformational leadership

Briefly, transactional leadership (or management) assumes that the relationship between people in an FE environment is a simple exchange for mutual benefit. People are paid to do a job and managers tell them what it is. Managers lay down accountabilities and the criteria by which staff are judged. If the people doing the job need to work harder or to change, then you may have to pay them more, and this will motivate, or at least compensate them. Orders are given and received, control established. For inexperienced managers, or those who are unsure of their ground, perhaps nervous of losing control or simply following the model of their own superiors, this can be assumed as the only model. Not being in control is not managing, and control means transactions to establish the dominance of correct procedure. It requires accountability and compliance.

However, it is in this sense that management, or 'managerialism', can be seen by staff as a process of worshipping process, a means by which individuals in authority protect their own job by making other people do things that satisfy the demands which an institution or some external body makes upon the manager. Staff fill in forms because it is your job to make sure they have done so. It has nothing to do, in their eyes, with education, or civilised discourse, or good relationships. Instead of shared values you have opposing interests.

Walker and Ryan point out that

> role culture is still the dominant organisational culture in education.... The assumptions here are that workers cannot be trusted, work only for instrumental gain, lack creativity, will not take responsibility nor show initiative and will resist change unless they are coerced. The result may be a kind of self-fulfilling prophecy, in that resisting change becomes one of the few areas in which staff can be truly creative.
>
> p150 of Ashcroft and James ed. (1999)

Also, as one should never forget,

> the loyalty of teachers is often to professional standards and the professional role, and not necessarily to the demands of superiors of the organisation (ibid 143)

and the nature of teaching – an individual entering a room full of other individuals then shutting the door and managing social inter-action, emotional and intellectual growth, is difficult to control from an office elsewhere.

> Teachers need to operate independently, with autonomy, because they work in an extremely dynamic environment. Teacher empowerment is, therefore, essential for facilitating day-to-day professional decision making. (ibid 144)

In the teaching context, there are so many ways that control is difficult to establish except over the least important functions. You can make people create lesson plans but can you make them teach well? You make them mark registers but can you make them create a class who actually want to attend often and on time?

For all these reasons, it is more cost and time-effective, more realistic and, in short, more civilised, to employ transformational leadership. But that has its own problems.

Muijs et al (2006) describe it as

> leadership that transforms individuals and organisations through an appeal to values and long term goals. In this way, it manages to reach followers and tap in to their intrinsic motivation.

and argue that

> ...in education.. a strong moral purpose and commitment among ... staff and managers, relative job security and low and Government-determined pay levels will tend to favour the effectiveness of transformational over more transactional forms of leadership in fostering lasting change. (p88)

Staff will then adopt goals on a personal level and be willing to "transcend their own self-interest" (p89). When staff in successful FE colleges were interviewed:

transformational behaviours were equated with leadership ... transactional behaviours were equated with management ... definitions of management tended to encompass an operational focus and be primarily concerned with meeting targets. In contrast, interpretations of leadership centred on values and vision for the organisation (96)

Also, as Lumby et al point out (2005) transformational styles assume that we shall seek out expertise wherever it happens to be in the organisation, not just in a particular formal role.

It has obvious apparent advantages. Transactional management assumes you motivate by pay. Pay is relatively low in FE. It has fallen by comparison with schools, and is difficult to increase for the majority even if you wanted to, so it cannot be seen as the main motivator. However, if we assume that education implies a "strong moral purpose and commitment ..... (with) relative job security" then an appeal to values may be more sensible when trying to foster lasting change (Muijs et al 2006, p88). Of course, this commitment may be to what teachers see as the students' interest as they define it, not as you define it.

The sceptical may argue that 'moral purpose' can create self-righteousness and be used to justify many forms of non-co-operation. Staff without responsibility for data collection will argue that they know best what is required and need to spend time talking with students and creating new material, not filling in useless forms. But what form of transactional management would actually alter that? You can make teachers fill in forms, but you can't make them care about the process that, according to you, requires them. And without sceptical feedback loops, how will you know if you are, in fact, being over-prescriptive and wasting time? What we are looking for is not a workforce coerced into activity, using creativity to undermine what they find tiresome or insulting, but a community of educators who share core values and a sense of purpose.

There is, of course, an apparent contradiction between the notion of a community or creative professionals and a strong leader. Walker and Ryan remind us of the perennial appeal of the parental figure who will make the trains run on time and remove problems from our shoulders

> ...in a climate of uncertainty and insecurity. There is often the desire for conventional (strong) leadership to solve all problems and dissipate all threats. - (ed Ashcroft and James p151)

But passively handing over responsibility to a leader is not the way to create a community acting on shared values to transform the learning experience of a disparate student body.

Strong leaders can disrupt an organisation only to engender passive resistance as staff "wait for the leader to move on" (Muijs et al 2006 p90). It is one of the under-appreciated facts of management that those who wish to exercise control are often less permanent than those who wish to remain uncontrolled. The passive resisters will be in post long after the strong leader has left to run an academy or become a consultant.

> In many cases, while leadership at the top is strong, the overall leadership capacity of the organisation has not been enhanced, leading to problems being stored up for the future. ... Authoritarian forms of leadership tend not to endure, with collegial processes best-suited to long lasting improvement.... (Muijs et al 2006 p90)

> While individual 'charismatic leaders' may deliver organizational improvements, this is often very short-term and followed by frustration or despondent dependency.   Collinson (2006) p7

And it is not easy for even strong leaders to make an impression, even temporarily. There is, as Muijs at al so delicately point out, a "limited pool of applicants" for the charismatic style, and even if you find one who is successful elsewhere, they may not be effective in a different kind of organisation

> Leadership does not necessarily transfer across situations (89)

and indeed,

> organisational culture is equally likely to itself change and mould leadership (89)

In fact, the size and complexity of FE institutions, combined with the strength of departmental/vocational cultures, will often mean more real power lies with the provincial barons in the annexes than the new king or queen in the central castle.

So, for all these reasons, whilst transformational leadership may be what is required, a simple strong leader model is probably not the way to obtain it unless change also includes a move towards distributed leadership.

In theory, this is a simple argument that a group of professionals, educated and motivated, operate most effectively for the common good when they share values and goals to such as extent that power can be diffused through the organisation. They control their own behaviour to achieve what is required, because they understand the requirements and internalise them. Or, perhaps, they find that the requirements that make an effective organisation have much in common with their own personal motivation and self-image.

Unsurprisingly, there are few examples of this in practice.

> Distributed leadership was readily associated with the distribution of responsibilities rather than power. It was viewed largely as a mechanism for delivering organisational imperatives. Muijs et al (2006) 97

> Distributed leadership is largely equated with team working and collaboration. It is often enacted as distribution of responsibilities to meet operational imperatives, rather than the distribution of power
>
> Lumby et al (2005), p24

> An alienated and demoralised workforce ... is not readily attracted by power-sharing.
>
> Walker and Ryan
> in Ashcroft and James (ed 1999) p151

This is familiar territory, where terms such as 'consultation' in FE are

> used more to communicate prior management decisions to staff than to involve them in decision-making. Muijs et al (2006) p90

So, because 'consulting' and 'involving' staff has been in reality a new terminology of control, not of empowerment,

> there is little evidence ... in this sample for the existence of forms of shared transformational leadership in the ten case study organisations (ibid 97)

even though the colleges they chose had a reputation for effective leadership. More importantly:

> What we cannot conclude from this study is that any particular method of leadership development, or indeed leadership, is more effective (ibid 193)

They can conclude that transformational styles are more popular, but also point out that there is unlikely to be one style that works in all situations. The 'normative stances taken with regard to leadership' should not persuade us that there is a right way, or a model to follow. Rather, it is likely that good leaders, or good managers, will be willing to adopt different styles according to context.

Moreover, all this focus on the power of a leader to transform the organisation that he or she is leading can lead to a romanticised view of the heroic individual, what Collinson(s) (2006) refers to as the 'leader as saviour'. This under-estimates the important question of their relationship with the followers, the people left behind when they have moved on, who actually comprise the organisation itself.

> Educational leaders are being redefined as 'chief executives', 'managing directors' and/or 'presidents' which reflects the way the sector is increasingly operating as a business, moving from 'welfarism' to 'new managerialism' (p7)

They argue for a

> 'post-heroic', less 'leader-centric' conception of post-16 leadership (p8)

and point out that the "policy of intensified scrutiny" and performance assessment can be counter-productive.

> It is, for example, possible that the kind of 'audit cultures' that increasingly characterise the UK education sector may reduce employee morale and increase mistrust (p9)

Everyone learns to play the game where targets are met, or apparently met, but the recording and presenting process becomes the main focus of attention, instead of the bringing about of more learning. In a sector where employees are supposed to be 'knowledge leaders' in the classroom, in would seem logical to distribute notions of leadership down through the hierarchy (p10). However, one of the questions they pose for their ongoing research is whether distributed leadership could "become a way for leaders to deny responsibility and to pass the buck to those in less senior positions" (p11)

The idea of a community of professionals might too easily become a controlling rhetoric, where people are told they are 'managing' when in fact they are merely being blamed. So when a student is not formally registered, or attending on time, or behaving properly, it is no use arguing that the MIS system was down for some of the previous week or that buses don't run regularly from that estate at 8.a.m. or the student hasn't eaten more than a doughnut since last night. Those facts are given, but changing student behaviour remains an imperative, with teachers or their manager being blamed if records don't show improvement. Put like this, it makes the process sound rather childish. Can a group of qualified and experienced professionals really be treated in that way? Wouldn't the organisation be more effective if there were realistic consideration of the variables in any challenge set? Perhaps the notion of distributed transformational leadership can be more easily approached through Collinson and Collinson's arguments about distance.

They point out that distance can be psychological or social, that it may have hierarchical dimensions and include physical distance (all leaders on the top floor and you're not, or the door always closed, with a PA to guard it) or interaction frequency (when did the LSAs last see the Principal?).

> Leaders may use distance as a form of power, or power as a form of distance (p12)

And in seeking a self-image of someone 'in control' they may be reluctant to share any form of authority, or to listen to the employee voice (p12). Chapter 6 considers this idea from the point of view of equal opportunities, and briefly looks at the idea that distancing is an essentially masculine process (albeit used often by women when trying to appear efficient to male colleagues). Handy reminds us that a major problem for any manager is the impossibility of concentrating on any task because of constant interruptions, a problem explored in chapter 4. But it is certainly clear that as distance increases, the leader becomes too detached to understand the audience to whom he or she will be sending "motivational messages" and the distance itself may create:

> back regions largely inaccessible to leaders .. in which employees construct counter-cultural practices (p13)

So, when they interviewed employees, they found a consistently strong preference for

> Clarity of direction, consistency of approach and willingness to take responsibility on the part of all those in senior positions .... widespread commitment to a distribution of power and responsibility, a strong preference to proximate (rather than distant) leadership styles .... leading by example. (pp18&24)

After all this, what does one conclude, and what is one to do about it in order to make any real improvements? As Socrates might put it - so what?

How to be better

Well, better at what? More efficient at meeting targets? Getting reports in on time? Keeping within budget and driving costs down? Keeping up to date with recent research? Making sure students learn more? Fuelling the local economy? Creating positive results from satisfaction surveys? Creating more pass grades or higher average grades? All of these and more?

As so often in any context involving social interaction, there is no single solution to any problem, even if we had a single definition of what the problem might be. There is no role model to follow, no recipe to apply. Organisations are large colonies of complicated people. You might, for example, create a well-structured, essentially fair and impressively documented Disciplinary System, only to find that it is applied and interpreted with such wide differences, all of which are justified at length by teachers in different vocational areas, that it becomes essentially meaningless as a college-wide process. But that does not necessarily mean the system was faulty or the people are being incompetent. It probably means that fairness is context-dependent, and in fact has been achieved in many cases. You just can't prove it very easily to Ofsted, but that is a separate issue, explored in chapter 3.

Likewise, good management, or effective leadership, or whatever you choose to call the thing you are aiming for, will only be achieved by flexibility and an intimate knowledge of the context. That is why models of leadership, and many training courses designed to provide leaders, sometimes seem irrelevant to over-burdened FE practitioners, who feel that generalised external solutions won't really apply to their internal problems.

> The most effective leadership development is perceived to be learning from experience, followed by mentoring and job shadowing. Effective development is seen as context-specific and carefully tailored to the needs of the individual and the organisation.
>
> Lumby et al (2005) p25

So, as this text proceeds through familiar contexts, looking at practical problems, it will make the following assumptions:

> Management is "the art of getting things done through people".[7] To harness what is positive and productive about those people, in a range of developing contexts, may require a range of different abilities and techniques, changed as appropriate; any manager who expects to follow the same style or recipe or role model every day is almost certainly doing something wrong. But the priority is to inspire, to equip and organise

---

[7] Mary Parker Follett, 1868-1933

those people so they operate in your absence exactly as they ought to, because that is what they want to do and they are capable of doing it. Hence chapter 2 on motivation and training. Teaching involves individual employees entering into a relationship with a group of other individuals, managing the social inter-action, emotional and intellectual growth on the basis of sometimes very unpredictable dynamics. What **really** controls that process? And what are the dangers when the language of commerce and industry is imported uncritically into educational management?

Teaching is not like any other business, and 'quality' is a slippery concept. Very poor performance in the classroom may be obvious. Barely adequate performance usually masks itself, because what is lost cannot easily be measured. How much more **might** have been achieved if the teacher had behaved differently? Cause and effect are complex so, unlike an ordinary production business, sub-standard work isn't easy to prove or to remedy. Everyone at all levels is accountable through printed records, but too often the collation of those records takes energy away from the process of improving what is being measured and harms the main purpose of the business. Hence Chapter 3 on paperwork and reality - the vital distinction between achieving and describing, making systems active, not counter-productive. How should a manager use evidence to inform and change behaviour? It considers ways in which information can enter and affect an organisation effectively, including ways to use research to improve practice.

Things will go wrong; if they didn't we wouldn't need managers. Education is about changing behaviour and sometimes behaviours, in students or staff or even in yourself, can be dysfunctional. Lack of time can lead to lack of control over even simple matters:

> Obviously you want your managers to be leaders but we've got leaders who are not managers.

cited Lumby et al (2005) p32

Chapter 4 looks at how time can be saved and stresses reduced, inviting a moment of self-analysis and reflection on working habits - managing time not marking time.

Curriculum design and financial management are intimately related, but sometimes in dysfunctional ways. Chapter 5 looks at issues affecting success rates and profit margins, assuming that a focus on the former creates the latter. Where should a manager's attention properly be directed in this industry? Can the manager of the Finance Dept. increase learning?

You will be legally responsible for a number of issues under the general heading of Equal Opportunities. Chapter 6 seeks to clarify such basic questions as "what is the real issue here? Who says so? What are we measuring and why, and what could/should we do with those measurements?" Equal Opportunities is not a just a phrase that involves collation of data and the ticking of boxes. More is expected from FE under the new legal frameworks and a proper response to them is also likely to be better business.

Similarly, the relationship of a provider to local and national employers is a question so fundamental to the business of FE that to misunderstand what is required or how best to manage it is to miss the point of FE altogether. However, to unpack the implications of that fact requires a more sophisticated understanding of what employers need as opposed to what some of them say they want, and requires of managers an ability to relate to external agencies with confident authority. What kind of authority has an FE manager in this context? How is it to be developed and deployed? How should a manager respond to labour Labour Market Information (LMI)? Do we actually know what makes people employable?

First, however, we need to return to the problem of what FE is for, and the role of the manager within it.

The clients for FE and managing in a network.

> Autonomy .... is not the most significant feature of the
> kind of relationship we envisage. We advocate and
> endorse something more powerful – a shared
> responsibility – across institutions and between
> institutions and the LSC in order to meet the needs of
> learners.   LSC (2002) p22

There can be very few people indeed who are not, in some
way or another, potential users of the services FE can provide.
There may be good reasons, outlined above, why a provider
would specialise and streamline the service, but at the same
time any healthy business will monitor its profile and keep an
eye on expanding markets. One thing all providers will have in
common is that they cannot work effectively in isolation, and
that is especially true now of a GFE college.

A single provider is part of a network for analysing what a
community needs and supplying that need. Whether the
'community' is defined as a small town or internationally, it is
not possible to gather the data and provide the range of
services effectively without an increasing range of effective
relationships, some of which are from people not normally
connected with education at all. This involves the manager in
working relationships across boundaries of expertise,
sometimes using unfamiliar language. The relationship between
providers and employers or unions will be examined more
closely in chapter 7, so we can start here by considering a
relatively straightforward relationship between two members of
the same industry.

FE is increasingly involved in HE, either providing it within
a local college or helping to attract more applicants for the local
universities. There are some interesting confusions here.

There is a governmental insistence that Vocational work
from 14 onwards, including any Diplomas that might be flavour
of the month, should be created by employers through Skills
Sector Councils (SSCs) or similar employer forums more

people should enter HE (at their own expense)vocational education should have parity of esteem with the academic routes.

One way to approach this question is to imagine more and more people going to university through vocational or work-based routes – apprenticeships leading to foundation degrees and so on, developing the skills valued by employers and not by academics. This is tied to questions about part-time or modular degrees. In trying to provide a flexible route, we are constantly hampered by worries about parity of esteem, and that has two elements. In trying to make vocational routes as respected as A levels we might be tempted to borrow elements from A level models, which is unlikely to be appropriate. A levels can only retain market currency by being awarded to a small percentage of the population. If you teach really well and all your students pass it will be said that the exam is too easy and standards are slipping. The system required failure to validate the passes. That assumption cannot be built into new vocational routes.

Whatever new models eventually gain acceptance, the process of developing them involves FE managers in new relationships with local HE colleagues and with employers. This may be handled through local forums or committees, through Life Long Learning Networks. It may require SMT presence for strategic planning and/or local practitioners to lead the way by example, developing pilots and staff development on the hoof. What is very clear is that providers cannot develop in response to governmental pressures without extensive networks, and that managers can only operate efficiently if their contacts and influence operate outside their own organisation.

Similarly, there are formal pressures to increase collaboration between schools, and between schools and other providers. This requires a manager from FE to be familiar with the agendas of and fluent in the language of a range of cultures from university common room to factory floor, school staff room to laboratory and commercial office.

Best (2006) refers to such links between normally distinct networks as 'boundary spanners' (p61) and there need to be more of them in FE as it develops. Some of the major clients for FE may have rejected learning or been rejected by it, or be representing those who have rejected it. The skills and knowledge required to liaise with local employers have little in common with the methods that work with local schools, probation officers, social workers or PRUs, or with the regulatory bodies such as Ofsted. Often, one is co-operating in public with business rivals and the freedom to manage is limited in formal and informal ways.

There are two issues here. One is about the degree of re-education we all require when engaging with new cultures. It takes time to meet and learn to understand such people. But even if you become personally fluent and persuasive in all those arenas, when you get back to base, will they follow your arguments? Unless you have involved staff in a series of exchanges at all levels, then any relationship between the institutions has to be mediated through you and may fail because you are the only one that can speak both languages – the others simply follow their usual agenda because they have not been privy to your enlightening exploration of new ways to relate. If you have made a new and important discovery, the first priority is not to share it but to arrange for other others to make the same discovery, so they also feel the need to act differently. Thus, effective distributed leadership would require links at as many levels as possible. The key terms is 'links', not just 'meetings. It requires joint activity or exploration to a purpose. A principal recently explained some of her college's benefits. It had partnerships with a football club which included sports training but also catering students staffing their restaurant at a new stadium. The college was taking over a local failing school to create a new academy. Exciting stuff. But how many of the college staff understood why it mattered, and why a portion of her time and the college budget would be redirected there, or, as they saw it, away from them?

Chapter 7 considers in more detail the problems of speaking with employers in their own language and chapter 3, looking at research, will also consider the language of HE, at evidence-based practice and its effects on FE discourse. Meanwhile we need to consider the people who constitute the community of learning. What motivates your staff and what kind of development would most benefit the students and thus the organisation?

Chapter 2

Motivation and CPD

how CPD becomes quality management
or
it's not about you, it's about them.

How society is conceived to be by its members considerably influences how it is
> Jarvie, *Concepts and Society* (1972) p69

The disconcerting truth (is) that where a conscientious teacher makes little impression, a self-centred, inflexible man whose idiosyncrasies border on the insane, can inspire his pupils with a deep and lasting love of the subject ... education is not and never will be an exact science.   Dr. John Rae, *Letters From School*

If the huge reservoir of tutor experience, altruism and professionalism were recognised and supported, improvements in learning would follow. This would entail creating more space for tutor autonomy and collaboration, encouraging, rewarding, sustaining and supporting creativity, imagination and innovation, and providing better tutor learning opportunities, including challenging their expectations and assumptions.
> TLRB (2005)

(CPD is) a logical chain of procedures which entails identifying school and staff needs, planning to meet those needs, providing varied and relevant activities, involving support staff alongside teachers, monitoring progress and evaluating the impact of the professional development. Overall, CPD was found to be most effective ... where the senior managers fully understood the connections between each link in the chain.

Ofsted (2006) The Logical Chain

Work-life balance is just something people talk about at work. And, frankly, they should all shut up.

Deborah Orr *Independent* 24/5/2006

It is sometimes argued that the qualities that make a good teacher don't necessarily make a good manager. That would depend on what kind of teaching has been taking place and what sort of manager one wants. Teachers have to affect the class in such a way they are persuaded to want to learn, to discover how to learn, to experience learning in a positive light and then deliver the results of that learning so they experience success though a formal certification system Then they will continue learning independently afterwards. Managers need to do something very similar with staff, except that staff are not replaced every year so you can't start again in September.

If management is getting things done through other people, and transformational leadership works by linking the motivations of others to the organisation's purpose, then it is important to understand what motivates others. Orr's point above is no less serous for its exasperated tone. Her argument was that the clichéd work/life distinction labels anything that happens at work as 'not life'. It demeans any activity at home as 'not work' and demeans activity within the workplace as if something you do whilst waiting for life to begin again after you leave. For most people, certainly within education, this is not the case. Work may provide a significant percentage of their personal satisfaction or even validation. Their work is extremely important to them, although that doesn't mean they take seriously all the statements made by their managers. A survey in 2006 concluded that dissatisfaction levels among staff in FE colleges varied from 6 – 75% but, more significantly, an average of 65% of managers thought morale was high whilst only 33% of their employees agreed. The causes of stress were less student-related than managerial, with less than half the staff feeling they were treated with respect. In the context of personnel management, feelings are facts, and you can't get things done through people you misrepresent in your mental model of the organisation.

It sometimes seems that college cultures have a lot in common with the old soviet regimes. Yurchak (2005) analysed the decline of soviet culture and identified as a key element the idea of 'authoritative discourse', roughly translated as The Party Line. There were official truths, announced in rather inflated language with tortuous syntax, and you had to learn the language in which truths were announced. After a while, people were fluent in the language and could speak it without bothering too much about the content of the truths, whether they were valid or even made sense. The language had a life of its own, and Yurchak cites a schoolgirl who was so enamoured by the impressive sounds of "serous and unclear phraseology" that she learned to reproduce them, even though "I would often be unable to explain what I wrote in my own words". She flourished in committees.

But it is not a simple matter. Some soviet citizens believed in socialism, but not in the temporary local manifestation they had to live with. They learned to make a mental separation between the formal language and reality as well as between the local manifestation and the ideal. They thought, somewhere, good ideas might exist, but meanwhile they turned up to meetings and voted for the resolution to maintain a quiet life, so as not to appear the kind of people who might cause trouble for their friends. Belief systems are complex and can often create contradictory behaviours.

All large organisations will have circulating within them the kind of jokes that used to be photocopied and are now emailed. They express, in humorous form, a degree of scepticism about the latest management fad, or about management in general. Best (2006) has several examples, one of which is taken from Sarason (1996), who took found it in general circulation.

Common advice from knowledgeable horse trainers includes the adage "if the horse you are riding dies, get off.". In the education business, alternatives include:

Buying a stronger whip

Moving the horse to a new location

Riding the horse for longer periods of time

Appointing a committee to study the horse

Arranging to visit other sites where they ride dead horses efficiently

Increasing the standards for dead horses

Creating a test for measuring our riding ability

Comparing how we're riding now with how we did 10 or 20 years ago.   Best (2006) p101

He includes other alternatives. I showed it to a manager in FE, a woman who takes seriously the fate of her students, and she immediately added "seeing if the horse is more economically viable if we put more riders on it." Everyone mocks management, especially management-speak, which is even mocked by those who use it every day. It is a sacred duty.

It may be, like Yurchak's soviet citizens, that people displaying those sceptical/cynical posters are idealistic believers in FE and willing workers for the greater good. They will probably carry out management instructions and could even have some respect for at least some of the management team. But they will still display the posters, because (a) they are good jokes, (b) most systems are bound to have an element of whatever is being mocked and (c) the grass roots perspective sometimes notices ironies and inefficiencies before those who created the system, and have their reputations and egos invested in it. They are declaring a natural solidarity with the workforce (= common sense) as opposed to those who tell them what to do (= followers of fads and users of management-speak).

It is worth remembering the sceptical view of management language taken by those who do not feel obliged to adopt it, especially when one is aspiring to 'leadership'. A YouGov survey in 2006 found 65% of employees in larger firms complaining of management-speak, with a third thinking thinking it betrayed a lack of confidence by the speaker and a fifth assuming it was trying to hide something. Many of the emailed or photocopied joke-sheets to which Best refers tend to assume that words disguise more than they reveal, and are not to be trusted. Once a word has been used too often, it becomes stale and tainted by poor examples. Such stale terms are easy targets for those who want to express dissatisfaction, and rarely serve a positive purpose, because the audience hear the repetition not the intention, assuming that use of the word is unthinking or devious. You will find examples for self-analysis in Annexe 1

Middle managers, of course, are in a difficult position. Bound by collective responsibility, they sometimes have to argue against a policy in committee then apply it anyway when they lose the argument. They may have to defend in public what they attack in private. Their language has to be more circumspect and diplomatic, but they do not wish to seem cowardly and dishonest when speaking with their staff. Some adopt a dual pose, trying to be one of the workers in the staffroom but then attending SMT meetings with a suit-and-tie expression. Dishonesty tends to rebound, but distinguishing it from diplomacy may take practice.

There is a certain kind of management training that involves filling in questionnaires to find out what 'type' you are. Just as students can be labelled as visual or kinaesthetic, managers may discover themselves to be, for example, a Machiavellian or a coordinator, a resource investigator or a great crested newt. Is your style democratic or autocratic, do you tell or sell, are you coercive or affiliative? As with the labels bandied about when discussing learning styles, they are misleading and even harmful if taken too seriously, but if taken lightly can be a useful way to start a conversation that increases self-knowledge. One set of distinctions is between the kinds of validation people expect or require at work. [8]

Some need the approval of superiors, and will work towards obtaining it to provide them with satisfaction. It is these employees that Keirsey (1998) has in mind when he advises that people like to be appreciated and they want the degree of appreciation to be proportional to their effort. Achievement "generates appreciation hunger" so an important management task is to provide proportional appreciation (p288). He imagines a teacher who will "will seek to be an entrepreneur" in achieving what you want, to get more praise (p 289).

That sounds as if they might be easy to employ, but when you are not there can you rely on them doing the right thing for the right reason? As Shakespeare's King John complained after his loyal followers had killed off an inconvenient young person on his behalf:

> It is the curse of kings to be attended
> By slaves that take their humours for a warrant
> *King John* IV ii 207-8

If you make a rule, or even mention a preference, however carefully phrased, some subordinate may apply it too rigidly to stay within their understanding of approved limits. The letter

---

[8] One example of this would be Belbin's self-perception inventory (Google free samples or see *Management Teams, Why they Succeed of Fail* by Dr Meredith Belbin). What follows is based partly on a distinction between formalistic, sociocentric and personalistic borrowed from Norman Dickie, who adapated it from T. E. Bier, *Contemporary Youth: Implications of the Personalistic Life Style for Organisations,* an unpublished doctoral thesis Case Western Reserve University 1967.

of the law is often more easily understood than the spirit, and weak managers or teachers at all levels tend to be bound too tightly by a limited understanding of the former.

Others need the approval of their peers. Managers need other managers to think well of them; teachers may prefer popularity in the staff room to your approval. They may disrupt meetings and be a more effective leader of opinion than the more-or-less 'external' manager who has popped in to justify the latest change in policy. If they are against an idea then you may find it difficult to persuade others to adopt it. If they are committed, they will bring others with them. They have, in Weber's terms, charismatic authority (which perhaps you would also like to have), as opposed to positional authority (which you have in theory, but which is sometimes not enough).

Some people express their personalities through work and their motivation is very personal. Work matters very much to them, but your opinion may matter less. If they are persuaded that something is valuable they will commit to it, even if you are absent. They may apply what they consider to be right even if you disagree.

Of course, as with learning styles, these crudely drawn 'types' may be tendencies and even moods. People are complex, and at the very least, a teacher may be a mixture of characteristics. They may act from a deep sense of personal commitment that overrides any concern with management approval, but still react favourably to receiving it, and be less effective if they feel undervalued. It is sometimes distressing to hear professionals talked about as if they are pawns to be manipulated by some clever management technique, as opposed to professionals to be consulted and reasoned with. Certainly, any technique is likely to fail if it is too obviously deployed. But, on the other hand, if teaching is manipulating classes for their own benefit then management has to include an ability to organise people for the common good. Chapter one discussed the need to revitalise teaching in FE and to encourage a more professional role after the effects of incorporation. Is there a form of discourse that would combine respect for professionalism with a sensible application of sound insights into group behaviour?

It is worth repeating that education is not a factory or a shop, and the choice of metaphor can be very important. It might seem at first that a lot of old management theory can be discarded as completely irrelevant. To cite only a more obvious example, Taylor's 'scientific management' [9] used time and motion studies to increase the loading of pig iron onto railway wagons from 12 to 47 tons a day. The language used in such studies is unlikely to motivate professional educators, but it may be that some ideas would be worth considering if duly translated. Taylor had to ask whether the workers would be more productive if they were dealing with another kind of coal, or a better designed shovel, which their managers had not considered. The important thing is that he measured the facts rather than arguing from a vague principal or lazy habit that took no account of them. The drive for evidence-based practice is discussed more fully in chapter 3.

Mary Parker Follet provides a more fruitful language, arguing that power over others is something that eludes you even as you try to grasp it. Her concern with democracy and citizenship emphasised the need to work with people, and to see power as something developed through co-operation, where individual effort is integrated to a 'universal whole' and personal differences are recognised by negotiation in this context [10]. Her ideas about conflict resolution and collaborative leadership may sound idealistic to someone worried about their authority and still traumatised by incorporation, but it is a language of common sense and respect which will in itself contribute to a more civilised environment. It also offers the

---

[9] Frederick W. Taylor, *The Principles of Scientific Management* 1911

[10] See *The New State* (1918) and *Creative Experience* (1924). Also *Mary P. Follet: Creating Democracy, Transforming Management* by Joan C. Tonn. Yale University Press ISBN: 0-300-09621-6. A full discussion of 'teacher types' is in the companion volume Teaching in FE (2013 ISBN-978-1482730876)

"Law of the Situation" - that there is no best way to do anything and all good solutions are local to time and place.

Often, you can only change students and their results through teachers. Changing the behaviour of teachers is not so different to changing that of students, so it would be ironic if teachers were asked to alter students by applying complex psychological insights then treated to the crude language of old-fashioned transactional management when it comes to their own motivation. Layard (2005) is an economist who reminds us that, even outside education, security is more important than income targets, so that incentive and performance-related pay doesn't usually improve quality. The experience of job-fulfilment, ownership, challenge and autonomy are more effective. His model is based on a more rounded view of human nature, one we might have a right to expect in an educational institution. If we can't do it, who can? FE staff could often earn more in secondary schools or in other industries. There is a reason they still work in FE and that reason, once you discover it, should be the basis of all actions that require or seek to increase their motivation.

Layard also reminds us of what all good teachers know - many assumptions about human behaviour and self-fulfilling prophecies. Tight supervision generates behaviour that requires even tighter control, so trust is an essential part of any manager/staff relationship. As Handy is quick to point out, trust can be misplaced and abused, but he also agrees that successful organisations tend to have more of it (pp 327-330, 374). Management is not about direct control, which is expensive and inefficient, but about internalising the organisation's aims to facilitate successful delegation. This requires:

A clear understanding of the limits of responsibility

A clear understanding of what would constitute success and failure (although not always strict limits on the method of achieving them)

A clear understanding of how and when the employee is to be monitored and held accountable.

This may be a brief conversation about a relatively small matter, or part of the annual appraisal system. Appraisals have been known to alienate the staff they are designed to motivate (or control). They can be seen as just another set of papers to be filled in for your benefit, not theirs. But they also provide a chance to find out what motivates each individual, so you can think more carefully about ways to internalise the organisation's aims. After all,

> While it may take some time to figure out how to adapt to the new management scheme, people can usually find ways around the constraints posed by innovations.
>
> Best (2006) p102-3

so if teachers do not adopt your aims as their own, then your aims may prove to be irrelevant.

Questions to ask about how your system works, or how you apply it, include:

> Is this a chance to discuss what makes the staff member feel engaged? Have you asked them what would make them feel more engaged?

> Have you actually asked them what motivates them? (They may say "money" which you haven't got, but may also accept that fact and negotiate alternatives which are, in fact, more important – like being asked such questions more often.)

> If the process had targets and staff are measured against them, how far do they feel those targets are personal and internalised as opposed to another

demand for your benefit?

Another caveat arises from the work of Day (1999). Referring to schools, he pointed out that teachers do not remain in the same frame of mind throughout their professional life. Although FE draws on a wider variety of staff, and often uses part-timers with professional roles elsewhere, it may still be useful to consider Day's model for a number of key phases in teaching careers, of "job stages" or "career-cycle stages" which affect potential development. These are:

1) launch a career with easy or painful beginnings
2) stabilise by integrating and consolidating
3) experiment with new challenges
4) reach a professional plateau (possibly stagnating)
5) final phase when interest contracts and disenchantment leads to an increase of outside interests

In the first stage, new teachers are socialised into a school or college culture. If they accept this culture, but find teaching stressful, they may internalise the reasons for failure. Alternatively, they may find it easier to blame the organisation, pushing failure away from them. But if they do accept the school culture, they may also accept a rationalisation for student failure as part of that culture (p60). Poor results will be due to widening participation, or poor parenting, not poor teaching.

The norms of the school or college culture may become internalised and unchallenged. They only become apparent when questioned. Any process of personal development involves self-examination, making tacit assumptions explicit (61). Therefore personal development involves to some extent challenging the institutional norms you have taken for granted.

Development inside any model of these broads stages will be affected by age, gender etc, but if we can identify the stages a teacher is going through we can personalise support systems. Like differentiating when taking a class, the sort of thing managers expect teachers to do all the time.

Interestingly, Day argues that a significant part of the explanation for teachers perceiving themselves to be at a plateau is the failure, in many schools, to permit teachers greater scope to know and relate to multiple classrooms, to see and work with other teachers. Thus, if the argument transfers to FE, as I think it does, part of any attempt to motivate staff would include encouraging them to network with others to learn from them. This is precisely the kind of activity that was encouraged by the QIA, and by the experience of IF in connecting schools with colleges.

Day argues that

> Conceptualisations of professional development as a linear continuum...are both over-simplistic and impractical, since they are not based on a 'teacher as person' perspective but systems, managerial perspective of 'teacher as employee'. (68)

He also points out that in-service training focuses on 'knowing what' and 'knowing how', which would use modelling, coaching and mentoring. They don't engage with personal growth, or take account of links between

> cognitive, emotional, social and personal development in the journey towards expertise in teaching (69).

So what would an appraisal be like if we did that, and how many of us are fit to carry out such an interview? How would you prepare to fulfil that obligation, and monitor that you are doing so?

Day's work was done with school teachers. In FE, with a much more varied source of staffing and strong vocational cultures, as well as a large percentage of part-time professionals who may be quite senior and/or experienced within their own fields outside your institution, there can be no single motivational factor or form of CPD which is suitable to all staff at all times. The IFL's insistence that all members should register their CPD on Reflect to remain licensed proved unpopular and was eventually removed, but evidence gained during the process suggested that (a) there was almost no activity that could not have a developmental effect if wisely reflected on but (b) most people still thought it terms of courses they had to attend. To repeat a point made in Chapter 1, Lumby et al (2005) found that

> The most effective form of leadership development is perceived to be learning from experience followed by mentoring and job shadowing (p25)

If managers and students don't always value hours spent passively in front of a speaker, why would teachers? If you want time to discuss matters with colleagues from outside your department or institution, why wouldn't they? Some colleges already swap staff so they can observe each other's good and bad practice. CPD needs to be considered imaginatively and realistically, asking what works, not what is easy to provide and record. For example, the British Council produced a bibliography called *Teaching Management Through Literature* [11] which suggests managers might read novels and plays then convene to discuss what they have learned about human nature. They recommend the method because literature, like good management, is about "gaining intellectual and emotional engagement" and provides safe ways to discuss potentially complex relationships.

Martinez (2001), in a study of college improvement, stressed that:
teachers and managers have different but

---

[11] selected by Ruth Herman 2004 isbn 0 86355 522 5

complementary contributions to make. The former provide high quality tutorials, targeted additional learning support and the rapid follow up of poor attendance. The latter provide support and programme statistics to enable teams to reflect on and analyse their own levels of achievement in areas such as retention. Colleges – even small colleges – are complex organisations of professionals who have a high degree of discretion in their work. Senior and middle managers identified a shared approach as the best way of ensuring that the whole really is more and not less than the sum of its parts. (p28)

If CPD is to connect with the reality of life as seen by teachers, it needs also to connect with the obvious fact that any improvement to the college as a whole has to be a team effort with shared goals, with a conviction that the people being 'improved' are part of a team with a shared responsibility, not just the problem on legs.

Martinez records that

> In contrast to the case studies written by senior managers, case studies written by heads of departments or programme or course leaders give much greater prominence to effective teamwork. (p29)

This is a matter of structure and of language, of tone and culture. As Lumby et (2005) point out,

> staff are likely to exhibit the same style of leadership as their manager (p24)

Moreover, there is little point running any CPD that does not help teachers to understand how it makes learning better, however indirectly. The "so what" at the end of any course, if it has to be a course, needs an answer in terms of classroom behaviour.

Management skills need to be expanded from an understandable concentration on finance and accountability to embrace a critical understanding of the central role of teaching and learning in the reform of post-16 education and training.

Learning styles and pedagogy in post-16 learning,
LSRC (2004)

It is essential to support and promote inspiring teachers to leadership roles.
Developing the Leaders of the Future: A Leadership Strategy for the Learning and Skills Sector, Summary of consultation conference, London, 22 October 2003.

An interesting development in the recent past was the move from advanced practitioners to subject learning champions. The latter are were formally organised through the DfES and enabled teachers to learn from each other but through a moderating central agency, but an early stage of development saw some colleges using Advanced Practitioners, an FE version of schools' Advanced Skills Teacher.

The teacher's experience – being an advanced practitioner

Mrs. A.

"We met as a group to decide what the term 'advanced practitioner' ought to mean. How did we want to see ourselves? We didn't want to be accountable to anyone in particular, in the sense that we didn't want to be seen as a kind of police force. Every college seemed to set up APs differently. Many seemed to be set up as a form of inspection, and a lot seemed to be overworked. We wanted to be approachable- if you're having trouble you can come and see us, ask "can you help us with this lesson?

Then, six months later, a new Quality Manager was appointed, and we were formally accountable to him. We'd already done a lot of training. It was slowly building up. Programme Area Managers volunteered their support and some staff approached us – mainly new members. New teachers are desperate and always open to new ideas. But the old lags were happy to talk to someone who was a non-threatening source of support, if they were faced with new challenges. They were happy to have us in their classrooms observing. The way they saw it, manager were not there to give them ideas, but we were. It was a different kind of relationship. We raised the problem of training for taking 14-16 year olds, of needing to be trained in advance, before they arrived. But nothing was done.

We had a two year contract, but when it ended there was no more funding. The remission we needed to carry on was peanuts – five hours – but of course, inspection was over now. The team withered away, which was a waste of expertise. It's difficult to quantify what we did and to prove the effect so you can argue for financial support."

Mr. B

"We finished at our peak, really. It's difficult to say if it was 'working' but people had started to approach us who hadn't before, it was growing.

We never had a clear agenda of what we were expected to do, so we made up our own. We held seminars and a summer conference to get visibility then people could feed off us for ideas – how to make classrooms more exciting.

We were set up to see people with low grades, so at first it was like a hit list. Later it was changed to a more voluntary basis. It was less threatening, more voluntary, and it worked better. But some people just refused to progress, and where did our power lie? Were we an arm of management or a friendly face?

> Our own management changed along the way – we never got any proper formal direction. If we were starting again we would need a clear focus and structure, although by now we could provide that for ourselves. But we needed a year to embed our own skills and to feel comfortable in that role.
>
> You need a wide range of vocational areas for the team – to cope with different cultures – but we couldn't cover them all. Although sometimes it was useful to have an AP from outside the college. After all, we are inspected from outside. You can compare groups and see what different people really mean by 'badly behaved students'. What was considered unacceptable seemed to vary enormously."

There are errors of management implicit in that example, several of which cohere around the general problem of validating experience. Cox and Smith (2004) argue that:

> Many good ideas remain unexploited in colleges because staff do not recognise their own good practice or lack opportunity to have it validated.

Also, although colleges may raise awareness of the material and good practice databases available through electronic sources, very few of them "monitor staff access to, and use of, these materials".

They found that good practice is most likely to be transferred from a familiar source, "when there is a close personal relationship between the source and the recipient of the practice" (p21). This may often be an informal process. However, if a good idea is to be more widely disseminated it needs to be somehow validated by the college.

Fielding et al (2005), looking at schools, also stress the importance of prior or trusting relationships (2.1) either within or between institutions as well as the benefits of having one's good practice recognised (2.12)

Of course, the conditions that allow a particular idea to flourish in one context may not exist in the place to which it is transferred, and in which it therefore fails. There is a difference between enforcing standard practice, which denies institutional and personal differences, and offering a package to be customised which has been previously endorsed. Good practice cannot be exported uncritically or without adaption.

Cox and Smith follow Showers et al (1987) in stressing the five stages of transfer:

Theory – a new idea is explained and justified

Demonstration – so you see how to apply it

Practice – so you can try it out

Feedback on how well it is working and finally

Coaching to help the teacher discuss the idea and try to improve it.

This is more sophisticated than just pointing people at on-line forums and good practice sites and it suggests more support and thus more management control of the process. The APs interviewed were concerned that offers of help, like appraisal systems, might be seen a form of control not a form of assistance. This begs several questions about the relationship of management to staff. Of course, offers of help may be seen as intrusive, controlling and unduly critical. But equally obviously, it is a management function to ensure everyone receives as much help as they need, which may be more than they want. The art of leadership is to make them want it.

Where teachers have themselves identified gaps in their practice, and actively want to make changes, they often really welcome input from teachers from other schools, especially when their assistance is personalised and customised.

One EAZ [12] supported teacher-led enquiry where teachers were encouraged to develop and share good practice through enquiry groups in which they chose their own areas of interest and the EAZ provided them with the time and resources to develop their work. This deliberately open-ended brief was seen as a strength of this way of working and had led to some imaginative and successful work, for example, looking at the use of sketch books in developing literacy and numeracy skills, zoning the classroom environment to cater for a range of learning styles or developing keyboard skills. The teachers who were involved in this work formed a network group in their own right.

In many cases this raised questions about the stakes involved in learning from others: that is, about the kinds of pressures teachers were under and their role in identifying their learning needs. Where individual teachers were under pressure within the school to improve their performance, on the basis of alleged 'failings' identified by others, the benefits of practice transfer activities were often, unsurprisingly, limited. One AST described a case where she had been 'imposed' by a head on a teacher who had been identified by Ofsted as poor; unsurprisingly the AST found it particularly difficult to transfer any practice effectively with this teacher. Should teachers feel deficient or lacking in any way, they may develop subtle forms of resistance.   Fielding et al (2005) 2.31

Despite some impressions, a website is not necessarily instantly accessible; negotiating one's way through it in order to find what one needs is also a skill. In our research we still encountered teachers who were obviously very new to electronic communication and may not yet possess the skills or confidence needed to

---

[12] Education Action Zone, now defunct. See also Aim Higher (ditto)

process the mass of information available on the
Internet.   ibid 3.24

There is a case for encouraging informal exchange through
relaxed systems in familiar surroundings. There is also a case
for validating and exporting good ideas more widely through
more formal methods. Subject Learning Coaches tried to
combine those functions. CPD within a college needs also to
get the balance right.

To begin with, this may require nothing more complex than
arranging opportunities to discuss practice and offering to
publish good ideas internally, through a CPD intranet or other
method. Even small ideas, however slight, and even small
improvements from a low proficiency base, are to be
welcomed. A culture of improvement requires a willingness to
improve, not an ability to be excellent – that may come later.
Examples may be excellent, but local applications will be as
good as they can be, and any application may be better than
none. Staff should not have the freedom to be lax, but they will
need "permission to make mistakes" (25) as they experiment to
try to get better. This is a CPD version of applying Maslow and
Bloom to the learning process. Make them feel comfortable
and set easy initial targets to build confidence, then stretch
them to a higher level of aspiration.

Another school-based project was Vitae, a "four year study,
commissioned by the DfES, which worked collaboratively with
teachers to find out from them the factors which affect their
work lives over time and how these may affect their teaching
and subsequent pupil progress and outcomes" [13].

A paper about this project presented to the BERA
conference 2003, again school based, noted that "asked about
changes in motivation over the last 3 years, half the teachers
reported a decline....there was a consistent decrease in
motivation over time as years of teaching increased" ...(at
secondary level) teachers who were deputy heads of

---

[13] www.education.gov.uk/publications/eOrderingDownload/RB743.pdf

departments were more likely to report that their motivation had decreased over the past three years (73.9%) compared to class teachers (47.4%), head of year (53.8%) and heads of departments (51.8%).

On 29th September 2006 the headline story in the TES was a further report on secondary and primary teachers suggesting that 80% of staff in the first seven years of their teaching life provide added value at or above expected levels. Between 8 - 23 years' experience provides only 68% and thereafter it is only 59%.

It is dangerous to transfer such ideas directly into other sectors, and to generalise when colleagues are all so different from each other, but it does seem that:

> 1) the more experienced a teacher becomes, the more stressful the job can become, so that constant support and invigoration is required to keep it fresh, although

> 2) managers can feel more stressed because, unlike class teachers, they can't shrink their problems of control to a single room at a time, with an agreed syllabus and material they create.

New teachers worry about entering the classroom; managers worry about leaving it, wistfully remembering the days when all their problems could be so clearly defined and contained, with some hope of a positive and measurable outcome. But perhaps the most significant finding by the Vitae project is that teachers are not consistent, and that many factors need to be taken into account when deciding which form of support or motivational action might work with an individual. The tendency to report high stress levels was highest in those with the most experience and 86.5% secondary teachers reported dissatisfaction with the time available for reflection on practice (89-90). Failure to expect stress, and to act in time to avoid it, can be expensive.

A principal once explained to me, shortly before he took early retirement, that there was really no such thing as stress if an employee was efficient. Stress was only pressure they couldn't handle. For example, if budgets are cut, then actions must be taken to retain standards within the new limitations. Managers are paid to do this. If they can't, because they don't know how, then they suffer stress. But that is no reason not to cut budgets. This view makes no allowance for middle managers, perhaps inadequately trained or inexperienced, who feel they don't know how to react to what they think of as a poor decision by their own line management, and do not know where to find guidance. Nor does it allow for the difficulty of teachers, who are asked to teach better for longer whilst seeing resources and reflection time cut by a system in which they seem to have no say.

In the economy as a whole, over 13 million days a year are lost through work-related stress, according to the Health & Safety Executive (HSE). To prevent this "epidemic", it has developed the *Management Standards for Work-related Stress* [14] and offers interesting case studies, several of which are from schools and a PRU. Nothing in them ought to be news to managers in FE. Once again, there is emphasis on having clear roles and responsibilities, feeling involved in decision making, understanding the reasons for decisions and feeling they are suitably prepared and supported to implement them.

Surowiecki (2004) claims that groups of people make better decisions than individuals, because they can pool experience and even out personal bias and weaknesses to produce a balanced and better informed view. There is wisdom in having a diverse team for that reason, and consulting them often. The more diverse the group, the more varied the input and points of view, the more likely it is that the decision will be right. Whilst it is a manager's job to be accountable for the effects of any actions with their sphere, they will have fewer wrong decisions if they consult and more effective implementation if their staff have internalised the aim.

There are probably policies in your college to deal with

---

[14] www.hse.gov.uk/stress with interesting case studies

stress, training, appraisal, CPD and all the other factors for which one needs policies when applying to Investors in People. But the difference between policy and practice, between the letter and the spirit of the law, can be large when a college or department has learned to defend itself with words on paper rather than apply itself to the problem. The next chapter considers some of the difficulties of operating a live, trust-based system with accountable and fully involved staff in an atmosphere where documents have been seen as masters instead of servants. It looks at the problems of behaviour – yours, theirs and the students – including ways to relieve stress in all three.

> Over-regulation and excessive administrative burdens distract and preoccupy colleges so that the learner and learning can at times seem like incidentals rather than the heart of further education.　　　　LSC (2002) p5

> Over-regulation can prevent a due focus on learners and learning and limit the time and energy which can be given to them. Because of this it has the potential to interfere with the learning process and drive down achievement. - ibid p 17

We can't say it often enough. But how would it feel to have learning at the heart of management? The next chapter looks at the relationship between paper and reality, between data and the learner's experience.

Chapter 3

paperwork and reality - using information to get results

Weak accountability, leadership and governance are common failings in poor provision. One of the most significant underpinning reasons why providers failed to improve was lack of effective accountability. Eight of the 13 colleges judged to be inadequate this year had inadequate governance. Self-assessment was inadequate in 14% of all learning and skills inspections carried out this year. In contrast, senior managers and leaders in providers that improved to outstanding set very clear direction. This involved setting ambitious but realistic targets to raise expectations for staff and all learners and ensuring that the provision offered was relevant to local contexts. Self-assessment was used very effectively in outstanding provision to closely monitor the progress towards targets and to evaluate and improve each aspect of learners' programmes, especially the quality of teaching and learning.

Ofsted, Annual Report and Accounts L&S Sector
(2011-12) 9

To accomplish renewal, you need to know what prevents it…there is usually no shortage of new ideas; the problem is to get a hearing for them. …. As a society becomes more concerned with precedent and custom it comes to care more about how things are done and less about whether they are done. The man who wins acclaim is not the one who gets things done but the one who has ingrained knowledge of the rules and accepted practices. Whether he accomplishes anything is less important than whether he conducts himself in an appropriate manner.
John Gardner, President of the Carnegie Corporation
cited Postman and Weingartner (1971) p24

If you put tomfoolery into a computer, nothing comes out but tomfoolery. But this tomfoolery, having passed through a very expensive machine, is somehow ennobled, and no-one dares to criticise it.
Gallois's Revelation from *The Official Rules (1980)*

They constantly try to escape
From the darkness without and within
By dreaming of systems so perfect
That no-one will need to be good.
T.S. Eliot *The Rock*

Data tells a story. Properly interrogated, it reveals the student experience, highlights dysfunction, suggests causes and possible remedies and informs intelligent decision making. Improperly used, carelessly defined or mishandled, it can alienate staff, decrease motivation and waste resources.

When students are first asked to undertake a project that involves 'research', teachers advise them how to balance hypotheses against evidence. They are told on the one hand not to be overwhelmed by useless facts and lose sight of the shaping interpretation, but on the other hand not to make statements without evidence to back them up. Teachers are then promoted to managers and seem to forget their own advice.

There is a general theme to the rest of this text which can be most easily referred to by the term dissociation. It affects both individuals trying to cope with their job and organisations failing to act efficiently. Dissociation is the act of failing to make connections, or even deliberately severing connections. It may be between words and acts, between what was said and the minutes of the meeting, between information and decisions, between the way things are and the way we would like to pretend they are. It means not facing up to the facts, or assuming we have them without bothering to check. It also includes, at the lowest and most simple level, the habit of mind that says sending an email to someone is solving a problem because, if they haven't replied yet, the ball is in their court so the problem has gone away. At the more advanced level, it includes quality systems that put all their energy into measuring the situation without any evidence that the measurements have led to improvement, or even to clarification of the problem.

This chapter begins with four related but different problems:

acting without the basis of proper information

owning information without acting on it

collating or demanding 'information' that does not serve any real purpose and

creating paper records that do not relate to reality as others would perceive it

Taken together, they deal with the essential arguments about quality and reform within FE, and with the vexed question of how managers organise their time so they can make progress instead of being constantly overwhelmed by events.

The Agenda for Change (DfES 2005) promised to

Sweep away the complexity that causes colleges to divert resources to collecting data of variable benefit
(p iii)

Collect only that data that colleges need to manage their own business (p vi)

Achieve a radical reduction in the bureaucracy and complexity associated with data collection and management information processes across the sector

So that data is cheaper to collect, and more likely to be used for

> effective strategic planning and performance
> management of the sector (p11)

That was good news, and there have been some improvements. It was a major complaint for some years that managers and teachers are constantly asked to provide and take seriously a set of complex measurements they didn't always consider useful for their purposes. But it is too easy to blame the entire problem on some governmental body. When Shakespeare's Brutus was complaining that Caesar was an unreasonable dictator, Cassius had to point out:

> The fault, dear Brutus, is not in our stars
> But in ourselves, that we are underlings
> *Julius Caesar I ii 140-141*

There are habits of mind common to most organisations and to all poor managers that allow time to be wasted because the right questions are not asked rigorously, and action is not taken. Bureaucratic contexts from outside sources only make worse a habit that can use the external agent as an excuse. The next chapter looks more closely at ways to manage personal time and offers an inventory of your own work habits with suggestions to reduce dissociation and thus stress. First, however, we need to put the problem in perspective.

In the early stages of my relationship with FE, a bluff Yorkshire-born Head of Dept. explain to me his two rules for dealing with an avalanche of paper.

> When it arrives, throw it away. Most of the time, it will never have mattered. If it is really important, someone with chase you later.

If it is not written down, it is not yet officially decided; if the ink is dry on the paper, they have already changed their minds.

Another experienced member of staff explained a filing system known as sequential stacking. As more stuff arrives, you put it on top of the old pile in the corner. If you ever need to refer to it (and mostly you won't) just ask the person who sent it how long ago it arrived, which will give you a rough location in inches above floor height.

These old-style responses are from the days when 'information' was something that just clogged the wheels. It was sent, filed, disposed of but rarely considered relevant to decisions. This was partly justified because the quality of the printed matter rarely matched the quantity, but also because the organisation receiving it had no process for employing it to inform their activities. Staff became used to the idea that reality had little to do with paperwork, which had to be shoveled out of the way. The recent reforms to FE seek to change that by improving the quality of both information and the decision-making process. A degree of scepticism is useful to that process.

Best (2006) is concerned at the way mere fads infest education. His perspective is American HE but his explanation seems to apply universally. There is a curve for ideas that are adopted and prove useful. The idea arrives at the bottom of the curve. The line rises as the idea is adopted then levels out at the higher plateau when it has become the norm. Fads seem to follow this curve at first, but then people become disillusioned and the line drops away again, falling back to where it started. In other words, fads are difficult to distinguish at first from good ideas, and seem to be adopted for good reasons, but just don't last. The problem is to avoid fads whilst not ignoring good ideas. Hula hoops, quality circles, total quality management (TQM) and Six Sigma are among his examples of fads that have passed. Male wedding rings and wrist watches are among the ideas that seemed like fads but caught on and stayed. If you could distinguish fads from good ideas at an early stage you could save a lot of time.

Of course, ideas come and go in any business, and you don't always have a choice but to deal with something imposed upon you by external authority. Were CPVE or TVEI a fad or a necessary stage of progression? Was the energy put into GNVQ's justified at the time or wasted when they were withdrawn. How much choice did any individual manager have at the time? More dangerous are the habits that managements tend to impose through the structure that seem to be the answer to a solution but are later dropped. One minute a new scheme is enthusiastically embraced and the next it is not referred to at all. Staff become cynical so the next new idea is treated with more scepticism.

Best argues that fads tend to universalise their solutions - they claim to have the answer to almost every problem - and among the methods used by fads to gain acceptance is a keen use of abstract terms. His examples include 'learning', 'managing', 'excellence', 'quality' and 'efficiency'. (p55), all terms abused by fads and eventually ringing alarm bells for those who may suspect that are used too often without precise meanings. Fads eventually fade partly because the over-hyped message gets boring, and the abstract terms have been devalued to the point where anyone using them invites suspicion. Worse still:

> Higher education administrators tend to copy management fads that begin in business or government. However, because colleges and universities aren't especially well-connected to business and government networks, they are continually laggards ... management innovations enter the world of higher education after they have already begun to be abandoned in the institutions where they emerged. (Best 2006 p99-100)

As FE continues to forge closer links with business, it may catch the diseases more quickly, which may seem at first to be an increase in efficiency. Perhaps it will be, but all workforces develop advance skills in avoiding any change they do not believe it. Unlike their managers, they have few reasons to lie to themselves about the fact that a fad doesn't work. Best reminds us that fads are bandwagons - some people will be riding them to enhance their careers. How many now senior FE figures rose on the tide of TVEI or IF or Vocational Diplomas? Egos and reputations will be involved, personal commitments made, so it is going to be difficult to admit that the idea imposed with such a fanfare upon the workforce was actually a dud.

> No perverseness equals that which is supported by a system, no errors are so difficult to root out as those which the understanding has pledged its credit to uphold.   Wordsworth (1815 Essay)

If we had an organisational habit of rigorously testing all new ideas at an early stage, the damage might be limited, but tests can be ineffective when intelligent people need to use words carefully to show they were right all along. And even after a fad has run its course and been rejected, it may leave behind effects that are dysfunctional. Best uses the figure of a spiral or a ratchet to show how fads come and go but we do not return to the point from which we started. He might have used the old terms thesis, antithesis and synthesis; even strong counter-revolutions against a fad will be tainted by the very thing they opposed, so that the next new idea will be affected by all the old wrong ideas, if only by reacting strongly against it.

Another of Best's examples of office folklore concerns American and Japanese rowing teams (p123). The Americans lost so a 'continuous improvement team' was set up to find out why. They found the Japanese had eight rowers and one steering, whilst the Americans had eight steering and one rowing. A consulting firm was hired to study this management structure and eventually concluded it needed to be reorganised. This led to the appointment of three steering directors, three steering managers and two steering supervisors, with a new performance standard to 'empower and incentivise' the single rower. They lost the next race by a larger margin, so they sacked the rower, sold the paddles and gave the money as bonuses to the senior executives. Sound familiar?

Cynicism is disabling and corrosive, but scepticism is a necessary managerial tool. Cynics know the price of everything and the value of nothing. Sceptics have values and believe in educational aims, but don't want to see students and teachers having their time wasted by sloppy thinking.

The key term in the twenty first century is "evidence-based decision making". As George Bernard Shaw pointed out, an idea is not responsible for the people who believe in it. No doubt, like all other phrases it will be abused and subject to poor examples that give it a bad name, but in essence it only states the very obvious but often overlooked fact that proper decisions require evidence, and this may be broadly of two types - day-to-day business information and research. Because our business is education, they are not always distinct.

Day-to-day business should always be done on the basis of sufficient information to inform decisions, and this might include, for example, student success rates broken down by department or level, the population of local schools by age to help predict post-14 or post-16 markets, job opportunities in the area, application rates for courses etc. It includes actually using the data available during transition, so students support can be set up before teaching begins. It would also include a habit of mind that always asks for the right amount of information from a trusted source before being willing to discuss an issue at any length.

> Aristotle maintained that women had fewer teeth than men; although he was twice married, it never occurred to him to verify this statement by examining his wives' mouths. He said also that children would be healthier if conceived when the wind is in the north. One gathers the two Mrs Aristotles both had to run out and look at the weathercock every evening before going to bed.
> Bertrand Russell, *The Impact of Science on Society*

Sometimes, it will be necessary to seek out information that is more complex than simple number-crunching, and to enquire after reasons and causes. Do some 14-16 year olds really learn more at college than at school? If so, why? Are there likely to be enough jobs for all the hairdressers we train every year? Do young black males need black male teachers as role models? Does an investment in CPD or learning styles or e-learning or free salads actually increase student performance? What is the largest single factor that might improve teaching in the weakest dept? Are we adding value to all the groups we teach? If not, who do we help the most each year, and why? Why do people drop out or fail every year? Is it inevitable? Do glossy brochures actually increase application rates and/or affect choice? What is the ideal length of a course information leaflet? Which job markets are growing and which shrinking locally?

The difficulty is that FE as a whole has not been used to gathering and using information as effectively as it might. Unlike HE, it was not used to handling large quantities of research. Unlike industry, it was not used to commissioning studies to inform commercial decisions. The collation of data it was used to seemed not to serve any real purpose, so staff became cynical about its value. The most important move in the 21st century is to persuade a cynical workforce to become dynamically sceptical, to believe in the value of information and to use it to question proposals.

Decisions and evidence

Manager A suggested at a meeting that the college develop a breakfast club to feed students as they come to college. She argued that diet affected behaviour, and that students would behave better and learn more if they were properly fed before classes.

Manager B, a cynic, objected to the potential cost of the proposal. He thought the claims for the effect of diet on behaviour unproven, and in any case not really their problem post 16. It sounded like another fad.

Manager C felt we took too little interest in the pastoral care of students and knew that many of them came from backgrounds where poor nutrition was an issue, along with a lack of parental support. He wanted to extend the idea by teaching them about healthy eating. He also suggested the refectory should not stock certain foods that had too many additives and should increase their range of salads.

Manager D asked what previous information existed on the success of such projects elsewhere. Was there any research to suggest that retention or achievement had been affected by diet alone and, if so, what were the cost/benefit implications in terms of the current funding system?

Manager E argued that much had been done in schools to try to use a management of student eating to control their behaviour. Research indicated that many factors came together to create the result, but that effects in terms of behaviour and concentration could certainly be encouraging. On the other hand, primary and some secondary schools had more control of what students ate, FE had much less.

Manager F happened to know there was a discretionary fund which should have been spent but, for various internal reasons, was still partially unused. The terms under which it was provided might be stretched to cover a breakfast club and it would do no harm to be seen to be active when inspectors were expected to visit next term.

The meeting was beginning to over-run so it was quickly decided to use the left-over finding to run a pilot in time for the inspection.

That conversation should never have taken place, because all the research should have been summarised on a single page of A4 by the proposer, with an annexe referring to sources if anyone wanted to challenge it. In fact, the research is very interesting [15] but sometimes couched in terms that would take

---

[15] detailed in chapter 5 of Teaching in FE.

more time to read than most FE managers can spare. If the team as a whole had been interested enough, they should have insisted on a summary to inform their argument. They would quickly have discovered that funding to feed Level 1 students had a much greater effect than funding aimed indiscriminately at all students, and that small factors such as providing free drinking water in classes throughout the day is also effective. But the decision was not, in the end, based on research or properly understood data. It was based, as so often, on the system called 'rearranging the deckchairs on the Titanic'. It looks like purposeful activity, but ultimately it is drowning not waving.

There are three movements designed to improve that situation. One is to provide better data and ways to use it, a second is to find effective ways to employ research and the third is to encourage a habit of mind that is less likely to decide anything without knowing what you need to know first, and demanding those facts quickly. That does not mean increasing bureaucracy, but reducing it, and reducing the dissociation that goes with it.

The first obvious point to make is that even the most excellent information is worthless if it is not read and used.

> Information systems can support improvement strategies as long as they provide wide access to data and accurate and timely information in a user-friendly format. The more widely college staff are consulted about the design and operation of quality assurance and information systems, the more effective such systems will be.   Martinez (2001) p38

It is not just a matter of gaining useful data, but of having a culture that knows how to use it, that **believes** in it. That journey, from justifiable cynicism to active belief, is the most important. For example, many FE staff have argued for some time that the way success in measured is unjust to their real achievements. Sixth form colleges and some schools will select carefully whom they enrol and then publish good results. They have done well with easy targets. FE, it is argued, tends to take in the more difficult cases and struggle to achieve what others will not attempt. They may not have such impressive success rates, but the distance travelled is greater and the journey more difficult. This argument begs several questions, not least the old habit of enrolling carelessly and setting unrealistic targets without sufficient support, but does it show that (a) FE is inevitably going to be unfairly treated or (b) it has been slow to make its case in public, which is a fault in senior management? The fault, dear Brutus....

A movement known as *New Measures of Success,* between 2005-7, made much of the notion of added value or distance travelled. Students entering FE have a point score and thus an expectation of success in various courses. If they have done badly in school but flourish in the FE environment, then the improvement will show and conclusions can be drawn. The mathematical process by which point scores are used to predict success (chances charts) can also act as a corrective to the tendency to enrol students in a course where their chances of success were always too low, so that realism can be enforced on the interview process.

The units of measurement used by schools, sixth form colleges and GFEs could be identical, and the points system used will include achievements in vocational subjects from age 14. Once understood, this system of employing data might be seen to answer many traditional objections and address perennial concerns. However, it can only increase belief and optimism if it is (a) properly explained and (b) employed as part of a whole-college system that uses the data to inform decisions, rather than parking it in a file that is ignored. The system will need integrity in order to contribute rather than detract. Moreover, the FE Choices website set up by the SFA focuses on pass rates and student/employer satisfaction questionnaires – the language of customer choice and value for money. It says nothing about distance travelled and the nature of the raw material we have to work with. Sometimes you have to promote the public perception of the data you wish to rely on to make a point.

The original newsletters explaining *New Measures of Success* had been circulating for over a year when I spoke with a group of FE managers who had not heard of it. In one case, it had been discussed between the Principal and the Director of MIS as a matter of data collection, but not with Directors of vocational centres as a matter for enrolment policy or a key element of their Self-Assessment and Review process (SAR). The dissociation between data collection and the way teachers behaved was complete, thus rendering the data not useful but a mere nuisance.

Of course, the information had been available on web sites. With any new initiative, there is usually a wealth of good practice available if you have time to look. There are newsletters from all the major information sources, if you have time to read them. Much of what you discover may not be relevant, some of it will not seem relevant until you have digested it and other elements will be relevant later but not yet. The difficulty is to sort wheat from chaff, and know what to read, at which stage. This is partly a time-management issue, which is considered in the next section, but it is also a cultural and organisational issue. Whose job is it to look up occasionally and see beyond the treadmill? To stop fighting fires and find out who is pouring on the petrol?

The manager's experience

Principal A is busy with financial matters, so assumes the Deputy Principal will circulate new information that is not directly to do with income and expenditure, markets and restructuring. That is what DPs are for. If the new idea is not obviously to do with these major issues, it can be delegated.

Deputy Principal B is a great believer in communicating. His newsletter tells staff about new ideas with exhortations to welcome them to 'drive up quality'. New ideas will always figure in his monthly sheet, along with amusing quotations. Staff are

---

thus 'well–informed'. He has many printed reports and newsletters in his office, and shows them to managers when allocating responsibility. He often does this when delegating.

Manager C is responsible for collating data about the new idea. It is her job to make sure official bodies receive on time the reports they require. She has received copies of relevant reports from the DP and is to report back to SMT when her draft is ready for approval. That is a source of pressure.

Course leader D is responsible for designing the curriculum and enrolling students. Not having read the monthly newsletter, he knows nothing about the new idea until Manager C asks for figures for the report. They are required urgently but it is not clear what it has to do with student learning. That is a source of stress. He solves the problem by doing it last and too quickly. Manager C is thus stressed and has to ask for improvements.

Teacher E knows nothing about any of this until he reads the DP's newsletter and hears the course leader complaining about how her time is being wasted. These negative associations are all he knows about the new idea.

For most colleges, one hopes this is a slightly old-fashioned example, because it is now essential for inspection purposes to show that data is used as the basis for planning and that self-analysis is encouraged throughout the organisation. But old habits die hard and changing the culture of a whole organisation requires a positive lead. All the responses above were reactive, and all tended to encourage a dissociation between what is important (making money, teaching students) and what is urgent (getting reports in), between systems and the people seen as their victims not their owners. Information and new ideas are not analysed and acted on in the sense that the college community understand the rationale. The idea is not associated with action until it has been reduced to an irritating act divorced from the original thinking.

In a similar context, the Learner Achievement Tracker will be less effective as a planning tool if teachers are conditioned by having ignored the old style Record of Achievement.

Students proudly carried them to interviews but FE staff tended to assume they would be anodyne or overly optimistic. Habits of mind caused by a weak system will sabotage improved systems unless managers take steps to show how the new systems can be used to solve problems that teachers identify as important.

It is unlikely any busy teacher or manager will be able to keep up to date with all the new ideas, and it takes both talent and experience to spot the important idea from the irrelevant or the fad. But the most important question is how the organisation is structured to deal with new ideas. Does it analyse them in terms of their effect on teaching and learning? Does it take seriously the idea that all staff need to buy into it, so it has to be introduced to them in their language and at their level? Is it a community of learning actively seeking to understand the new idea or a bureaucracy trying to protect itself from criticism?

It is in the latter context that quality assurance processes only encourage low-risk conformity. People do what they have to and keep the rules, but they don't actively explore and take risks to try to be better. You don't fatten a pig by measuring it; there is a vital distinction between describing and changing. Measuring takes time, and if that is all it does the time is wasted. Systems need to be active, not counter-productive. That is why a major element of the recent reform focuses on feedback loops, on how information is to be used. And it is why inspections need to be seen as a useful contribution to good management, not the impetus for defensive mountains of paperwork to cover over the cracks.[16] The people acting as

---

[16] Ofsted's survey of all inspected schools shows that overall, four times as many of the responding head teachers inspected in 2002/03 (66%) indicated that the benefits of inspection outweighed the detrimental effects than vice versa. This ratio had increased since 1998/99. Sixty per cent (rather than 40% previously) felt that the inspection had more beneficial than detrimental effects, 14% (compared with 22% before) felt that the detrimental effects outweighed the benefits and 25% (a reduction on the 37% formerly) felt that they were evenly balanced - Oftsed (2004) 98

managers now were often socialised into a system that reacted defensively to information. In changing themselves, they need also to socialise the next generation. It is part of a manager's job to create the culture that grows good managers.

The old ALI guide to learner-centred self-assessment advised that

> As the adult learning sector moves from external quality assessment to self-regulation, inspection has made a similar shift. Inspectors now look carefully at the quality of the providers' self-assessment processes ...
>
> You need to have systems and processes in place to collect evidence and it is important to ensure they are easy to understand and straightforward to use. Remember that you need sufficient evidence in your self-assessment report – but only sufficient – to ensure that your judgements are sound.
>
> ALI (2006) Intro and p21

Acting without analysis and evidence is dangerous; collecting evidence without acting on it is more dangerous. It is in this sense that FE can learn from business, where the culture of a successful enterprise will have taught employees to value analysis and research which is cost and time-efficient, and which earns its keep.

> To know and not to act is not to know
> Wang Yang-ming (1472–1529)

Research implies development, but a great deal of research still arrives in FE - if at all - from HE sources. It is then ignored because:

> Managers don't have time to read it.

Even if they did, they don't have the training to analyse it critically and imagine how to apply it.

Even if they did they don't have the time to think about how to apply it.

Even if they did, they are not in a position to apply it.

One of the dangers of starting to read research is that it tends to disable before it can enable.

> A caterpillar in the sun
> Was happy till a toad begun
> To ask: "Which leg comes after which?"
> And left her wallowing in a ditch
> Considering how to run[17]

Sometimes, stage one is to realise how much you didn't know and how wrong you were. Not everyone survives to the stage that helps to provide positive ways forward, especially if the research criticises habits dear to the reader's line manager. Exploration of this kind is less likely to benefit an organisation if undertaken unofficially or by an individual. It needs to be an integrated part of the formal quality system, so that insights have validity and an audience at SMT, even if they are initially uncomfortable.

> Policy makers have tended to utilise research findings when they have fitted with the political ideology predominant at the time. Where this has not been the case research findings have tended to be ignored or, in extreme cases, vilified (Hallam 2000)

---

[17] There are various versions of that verse but I have been unable to trace the author of this one. If anyone recognises it please inform info@bpfe.org.uk

Research may be dismissed for many reasons, not least a previous acquaintance with annoying nonsense passing itself off as educational research:

> One might well believe that most of 'the literature' is, in fact, hopelessly muddled and often unintelligible, riddled with doubtful assumptions and jargon-defended theories; the product, it might appear, more of fashion and fantasy than of any real concern for truth. One might even believe that it was not clear whether there were any 'authorities', or at least that it was not clear who they were. That is, in fact, my own view.
>
> Wilson (1975)

Most teachers will pick up ideas and try them out eclectically. They will find that some work and retain them, but rarely refer to educational theories to justify or explain them. They may be good without knowing why. (Smith 1973, Jarvie 1972). Most managers have long ago stopped reading any theory about teaching.

Even when it is read, research may be dismissed as "following an agenda set by researchers and irrelevant to practice" (Stanton 2000) and a lot of research based on schools is not directly applicable to FE because of the more varied student body. For example:

> Some FE students might best be described as clients of the organisation and, indeed, many colleges now have functions such as 'client services'. At its best, this means that colleges adapt to students' needs, rather than asking them to fit into the college's arrangements. However, some full-time students would rather think of themselves as belonging to a college, having influence through this membership rather than through their purchasing power. Both outlooks have to be catered for.
>
> Stanton (2000) p181

Moreover, one way that researchers remain employed is to think of new ways to disagree with each other. Seeking authority to inform practice, teachers and managers may find opposing points of view and, instead of consensus, an opposition of theoretical perspectives where discourse may be "spiteful, even warlike" whereas the least we might demand of them is to integrate their own warring conceptions of 'learning' to give us an agreed starting point (Desforges 2001). And, of course, it is actually very irritating when engaged in a difficult task to be told by someone who isn't how you are doing it wrongly

> On the outskirts of every agony sits some observant fellow who points.   Virginia Woolf, *The Waves*

One is naturally tempted to tell them where to stick their pointing finger.

It is also short-sighted to imagine that teachers or managers can ask research for a set of tips or techniques they can use immediately in practice. The process of applying new insights may involve re-thinking how one acts, and how to conceptualise the learning process:

> Practice is not simply something that the practitioner does, it is as much what the practitioner is, for practice is a constituent of the identity of the practitioner. Moreover, in as much as practice entails interpretation, reflection and transformation, it cannot be legislated for in terms of strict rules.
> Bloomer and James (2003) p249

Once research has suggested a way forward, the process of applying it is not just a matter of taking away a recipe.

> The tasks are both to interpret the findings in relation to real-life contexts (subject area, learner age groups, qualification levels, local socio-economic conditions)

and to manage complex development strategies to bring about change. These strategies themselves may then call for researchers again to monitor and evaluate the change strategy and advise the developer accordingly.

Morris and Stanton (2000)

And the final stage of any 'action research' ought to be that

> The organisation acknowledges that the process is cyclical and ongoing.

> The organisation needs to ensure achievements are sustained and that new improvements are planned or that current changes are refined.

> The organisation makes results public in order to facilitate transferability to other areas of its work or to influence developments elsewhere.

In which case

> The framework for action research fulfils all the requirements of a quality improvement cycle.

Smith (2004)

So the HE research community has a job to do in reforming their own practice to make it capable of enriching FE, and FE has a job to do in making itself accessible to ideas and knowing how to use them.

Notwithstanding all those caveats, it can still be argued that reading someone else's research will save you time because

> They have already done a lot of work and spent a lot of thinking time to reach conclusions you need to consider.

> You could easily spend a long time travelling in the

wrong direction if you don't know what has already been researched.

Some basic facts and caveats can avoid that, and we might distinguish between

Major research published in learned journals and books. They take time to find, time to read and some may already be outdated by the time they are published.

Working papers presented at conferences. They are sometimes more easily digested and are more likely to be of the moment, although a lot of the IF research, for example, was based on the first cohorts. By the time papers about them were circulated, the colleges had already learned their lessons and changed considerably. They were then offered research papers describing a reality that was sometimes two or three years out of date.

Papers and Guides published by bodies within the sector.[18] These will usually be succinct and focused on practicalities, but are unlikely to deviate too far from the broad sweep of the dominant ideology of the time.

Research commissioned by a manager to inform a local purpose. The various sources of IF funds in the early stages often included a small sum – around 7.5k - to pay for 'research'. This was very loosely defined and might, for example, be used to pay teachers and LSAs from FE to visit schools and bring back their insights into the transition process, to inform the management of behaviour and learning.

---

[18] past and present examples might include LSN, AOC, S4S, LSIS, LSDA, DES – delete as appropriate but see bpfe.org.uk/links for live links.

Recent developments include better organisation of routes to useful research papers and closer links between FE and HE as they start to combine programmes and training for senior managers, so that in future Principals are trained and qualified to employ new ideas more efficiently. As we recover from the excessive focus on narrowly-defined financial management caused by incorporation,

> Many of those working in FE colleges would agree that some kind of step change is necessary if teaching and learning are to regain the attention they deserve. Research is likely to be part of the solution, though as many of the participating ... tutors have said, it may not be research as is currently understood in many colleges of further education. - James ed. (2004) p58

It might, for example, involve short-term collaboration where teachers in schools and FE visit each other's classrooms and compare notes on what they learned about the learning contexts. It might involve teachers in different contexts using "collaborative journaling" (see Alterio, 2004) where they reflect together on matters as they arise or collectively analyse a topic of current concern. It might involve a team consisting of teachers, students, caretakers, LSAs and personal advisers inspecting the campus and the college literature to advise on equality of access, or marketing and student support staff talking with local voluntary organisations about unmet needs in the area. It might see teachers reading academic research and or sharing materials and/or taking part in seminars to reflect on practice through their working lives, overseen lightly and creatively by a CPD manager who understands that professionals need to be trusted to find their own solutions, and to be held accountable for the results.

Very poor performance in the classroom may be obvious. Barely adequate performance usually masks itself, because what is lost cannot be easily measured; potential is rarely a simple mathematical fact. Cause and effect are complex so, unlike an ordinary factory production business, sub-standard work isn't easy to prove or to remedy. Good management finds a way to relate standards to personal responsibility and to evidence. But, of course, it can only do that is the manager is acting effectively. The next chapter looks at personal working habits to provide an inventory and a survival guide.

Chapter 4

Managing time, behaviour and stress

> There is always the danger that people who work hard
> become blinded by work itself and, by a paradox, lazy-
> minded.   V. S. Pritchett, *Midnight Oil*

> The inner spirit of bureaucracy lies in the exciting
> interplay of non-ideas and the effervescent sparkling of
> human personalities engaged in non-directive pursuits
> .... When in charge, ponder. When in trouble, delegate.
> When in doubt, mumble.   James H.Boren

Tommy Cooper used to tell the story of going to his doctor
to say "It hurts when I do this", to which his doctor wisely
replied, "Well, don't do it then." Sometimes, it is that simple.

Other advice passed on through the years includes the pair
that run (a) get off your arse and do it (b) look before you
leap. If you think (b) invalidates (a) you haven't understood the
idea of active research to inform decision making. Also, put
very simply:

> When you are afraid things are going to get worse if
> you don't do something it can prompt you into action.
> But it is not good when you are so afraid that it keeps
> you from doing anything.
> *Who Moved my Cheese?* Spencer Johnson

Having explored the wider context of national data and the
potential of applying research to practice, it is worth running a
simple health check over your own working practices. This
chapter considers the functional skills for managers, and
techniques for acting efficiently. Such advice can sometimes
seem condescending or simplistic, but sometimes the truth *is*

simple. It is always possible to find complex rationalisations for ignoring it.

There are several traits one can identify among managers in FE, including management by busyness, management by presence and management by promises.

Management by busyness involves always having a pile of papers on the desk and a full diary. Sequential stacking instead of selective disposal means having an impressive workload clearly visible for all to see. It is a badge of office, proof of importance, to be surrounded with work. Its practitioners will say, partly in jest, that a clear desk is the sign of a sick mind. But looking important also involves feeling worried.

In 2005 Common Purpose found that management in general, over a variety of industries, suffered a "deficit of courage." Doubting their own judgement and feeling untrained and under-supported, they avoided challenges at work (66% middle managers, 59 % at board level). Among the ten most common challenges was dealing with difficult personalities, giving and receiving criticism, negotiating with people outside their authority and making judgements under time pressure. A common reaction to such fears is to hide from them, keeping busy instead with tasks that appear to be important but are within the comfort zone. It is easy to be busy, more difficult to refuse the excuse and remain focused on what really matters.

A related problem is management by presence. – a version of macho management that means getting in early and leaving late – always being around because the job is so pressurised you need very long days to cope, and even then it is never quite in control. There is a positive version of this. Some people are early birds and some night owls. There is a pleasure to be gained in missing the rush hour by cruising in early, brewing up and listening to mellow sounds on your speakers whilst slowly preparing for the day before anyone arrives to spoil it. Equally, there is pleasure to be gained by tidying the desk, reviewing the day, preparing for the next morning and slowly toddling off to a local bar to exchange informal chat. Being first in or last out is not in itself a problem, and may be a sensible adaption to personal biorhythms. Being first in **and** last out is an indication something is wrong, particularly if the result is that deadlines are still not met. The pressures will be there after your funeral is over. Will colleagues attend the wake and remember you as someone who actually got things done, or just someone who was always busy?

Unlike some jobs – building a house, climbing a mountain or writing a novel – there is no such thing in educational management as an obvious finished product with a possible rest time afterwards. There used to be academic years with long summer breaks during which one could feel that one group had left and another hadn't arrived yet. That rhythm has been reformed out of existence. There are still individual projects that start and finish. But, in general, the pressure is continual because there is always something else to be done with no sense of completion or achievement that allows a natural break before going back into the ring for another round.

Using time

Manager A was in the building before the cleaners left. Crossing from one annexe to another, he met a colleague in the car park and in conversation bewailed the fact that the workload never seemed to reduce. It was unreasonable to ask for so much in such a short time. Later that day, he was observed in the admin office, making a similar complaint. By adding up all the hours he spent bewailing his lack of time, he would have gained a day a week extra to actually do something, but would probably still not have enough time. The pile of papers would not be read, the report not written, the strategy not finalised. But he would be putting in the hours.

Manager B focused on achieving the obvious ends. She gathered up documents and read them on the train. Finished products emerged from her office. This left little time for speaking with her own staff, but she managed to delegate some tasks and keep them informed by sending our newsletters and

---

briefing them at fortnightly meetings. At the end of the year, with a stack of finished reports to her credit, she was surprised to discover that much of what she had written was unread and unimplemented. The question most often asked by her staff was the one she had not considered; the major objection emerging from her line manager was one she had not foreseen.

Another problem with management is being unpopular. Under pressure of time and constrained by budgets, you cannot deliver everything that staff require, or demand. You would like to, you intend to and you promise to with the best intentions. Later, unable to deliver on that promise, you are even more unpopular, and considered weak. Saying no in the first place would lead to less unpopularity. That requires a clear vision of what is truly possible and the strength of mind to face down dissent if it is based on unrealistic expectations. This is easier if you have moulded a team who have internalised your aims and understand the context for decisions, but sometimes the options are all unpleasant.

Pressure is something you need to manage – it is what you are paid for. Stress arises when pressures are not managed. This may be because you have not found a way forward or a suitable working practice. It may be because choices are between the unpleasant (create redundancies or expel a student) and the very unpleasant (have them created for you or wait for the next explosion of violent behaviour). The answer to the first kind of stress is not to manage it but to remove it. Only the second kind should be 'managed' in the sense that it is accepted, and then only temporarily. [19]

---

[19] Management standards for work-related stress at http://hse.gov.uk/stress/standards/

Facing facts

Manager A asked for support from a time-management consultant. After extensive discussion, it became clear that nothing was glaringly wrong with most of her working practices or management techniques. She just had too much to do. She said 'yes' when she should have said 'no'. Her workload was unreasonable. Therefore, she was being badly managed. Her solution was to renegotiate her role and workload with her own line manager. This proved impossible – she was badly managed – so she left.

Manager 2 was faced with a number of disciplinary problems among students who were at times disruptive, loud verbally aggressive and potentially violent. There were few students in the class and it was not economically viable without most of its members. The course tutor was not particularly effective in her role, but it was agreed among other teachers that even if she were to improve, the problem was now beyond most of them on days when behaviour as at its worst. Some were part-timers who needed the income but would otherwise have left. Considering how to react, the manager called a team meeting to discuss it. The first time all members of the team could be free to attend was in 8 days' time. Five days later, a student was assaulted in class and the perpetrator automatically excluded. Two others ceased attending. The class was closed by her line manager. The part-timers had to be paid until the end of the termly contract.

The stages in solving any problem are broadly similar:

> Decide if it is yours

> If it is, decide what solutions are possible and preferable

Decide how best to implement the preferred option
Take necessary actions in good time

Check on the result

Ask what you can learn from the experience

So the first stage in solving a problem is to know what kind of problem it is.

Some problems are so inherent in an organisational culture that the only real solution is to change that culture or to seek out another to work in. The latter is more likely to succeed on the basis of a successful track record. Meanwhile, whether or not you consider yourself well managed in the short term, pressures need to be managed to avoid their becoming a source of stress or, if that is not possible, stress needs to be managed in itself. We shall approach the final option only when all other options have been considered.

1) Decide if it is yours = analysing and owning the problem

Suppose you delegated authority then the member of staff comes to you with a problem (A) which they can't handle. If you take it away from them there was no point delegating, so your problem (B) is to help them grow enough to deal with it. Unless of course, you realise you made a bad decision in appointing them, in which case you have problems (C) and (A) to solve. Just solving (A) will only mean getting problems A2 and A3 later on.

There may be good reasons why a problem should not remain on your desk or in the forefront of your attention. First, you need to employ the traditional means of ascribing importance and urgency. The four heading, which you have almost certainly seen before, are

Important and Urgent = priority 1

Important but Not Urgent = priority 2

Not Important but Urgent = priority 3

Not Important/Not Urgent = priority 4

Would you agree with these examples?

Important and Urgent priority 1	Important but Not Urgent priority 2
There is a meeting to address soon that needs an agenda or presentation or a plan of action to make the most of the opportunity A report to a funding body or a disciplinary meeting is due soon There is a crisis – a class with no teacher or a course due to start with insufficient students, a source of dissatisfaction that is about to come to a head without your controlling the dynamics Bills have not been paid. This may include something apparently minor, like appearing at an event just to show support. If not appearing will cause significant loss of morale,	Strategic planning – long term at the moment but if not done will become urgent, or be too late. A crisis will build up if you do not prevent it by proper planning, so you need to set your own deadlines. Move them if necessary for priority one cases, but not for any other. This may include checking research, collating data or time-out for team-building or morale management. That is justified if you can clarify to your own satisfaction the purpose and likely benefit of the time spent. You may need to hone your skills in skim-reading or consulting – see below under 'assertiveness'.

then it may belong here. Take breaks and have lunch – see below under 'managing your own mood'.	
Not Important/Urgent priority 3	**Not Important/Not Urgent priority 4**
Interruptions will vary. Some call for instant response – injured students are priority one but aggrieved upset staff may be better dealt with another way. See below under 'listening'. Phone calls and letters may or may not require action now. If they do, and can be quickly turned round, then dealing with them will give you a sense of achievement and control – priority one, if not necessarily top of the list before lunch. Otherwise, they can wait until something more urgent has been achieved, then cleared as soon as possible.	If the calls or letters or interruptions are neither urgent not important, refuse them. Get a spam filter, train your secretarial help to filter messages, close the door and do something more worthy of your expensive time. If the task is easy it might be tempting to do it first for that reason, assuming you will gain a sense of achievement and control, but if it lies in this box then is it actually not worth doing at all when more difficult tasks are still unfinished? You could delegate it, but is it worthy of **their** time? You can fill up a day with priority four tasks. If it is all you have to do, you are seriously underused. If it is not, why are you doing it?

It shouldn't need saying, but often bears repeating that sending an email is not achieving anything. Getting a reply/response is doing the job. Sending words on the easy way is often just passing the buck or buying time. The statement "I sent an email and I'm waiting for a response" often means "I passed on the hot coal and am now blowing on my fingers".

Similarly, you need to be honest with yourself about your real motives. It is necessary to get out of the office, partly to take a break but also to see what is happening in the areas for which you are responsible. It is therefore good practice to notice when you have been churning out paperwork for hours and instead go for a walk about in your area. You won't be detained long – you are obviously en route – but you will return refreshed and informed. However, there is also a brand of manager who revels in personal contact, is good a 'people skills' but just doesn't like paperwork. If you are honest with yourself, how far is your balance of private/public time based on defensive reactions?

You will often be advised by time-management texts to make a 'to-do' list. It is necessary to prioritise your tasks and making a list helps you do so. However, making a list is not the same as actually completing the task, any more than sending someone an email is the same as getting a response from them. Lists and messages are useful, but responses and actions are what you need to be able to cross something off the list.

In analysing the task, you will also need to decide whether or not to delegate, and this can be in three directions – up, sideways or down. There are two kinds of problem – those you own and those you do not.

Referring upwards - it might come back to you for action but first the problem needs to be acknowledged and approved at a higher level. Record what was said, to whom and when. Until it comes back, you do not own it.

Referring sideways – if it is their area of expertise or formal accountability not yours, perhaps you should not trespass. But record what was said, to whom and when. You may be able to collaborate if it is in your interest that something happens, but who owns the problem if nothing happens? Who suffers from inaction is not the same question as who is accountable for the action, so it may need to be referred upwards first and then back down to someone else. Unless formally given to you, you do not own it, even if affects you.

Referring downwards can take place when a member of staff is capable and might be interested. Both need to apply if delegating is to work. If you delegate the task, do you also delegate the role/authority? Do they attend the next meeting on their own, come with you or hand over the report for you to present? If roles become unclear then delegation is harder to achieve and it looks more like exploitation. Is it really your job or is it properly **acknowledged** as theirs? Once delegated, how closely do you need to monitor the process before it comes back to you as completed?

Can the delegatee hand it on lower down the pecking order? If so, why didn't you? It is good to give responsibility to encourage initiative but you need to distinguish between Team Building and Teflon. Some people accept a task and immediately ask another to do the work. Others use delegation to build the confidence and experience of junior members of the team. Do you know the staff well enough to spot the difference?

2) If it really is your problem, decide what solutions are possible and preferable

The previous chapter commented on the need for research to clarify the dynamics of any situation and data to inform decisions. Argument needs to be evidence-based. What is not always appreciated is the degree to which research can sometimes open our eyes to solutions we may never have dreamed of. The phrase 'blue-sky thinking' is one of those annoying buzz words Best (2006) might have chosen as being devalued by faddishness and likely to alienate anyone invited to partake in it. You may prefer the notion of playfulness. March (1985) argues that we sometimes need to re-examine our goals and be creative is escaping from old notions of what we need to take seriously, inventing new goals. Playfulness is the temporary suspension of rules. That frees us from the blindness of habit. His rules for such a process are:

> Treat goals as hypotheses
> Treat intuition as real
> Treat hypocrisy as transition
> Treat memory as enemy
> Treat experience as theory

Organisations can be playful even if the people in them are not, by varying the degree of control exercised and allowing temporary relief.

The manager's experience

A tired army marched slowly towards the horizon. The general worked night and day to ensure they had water and food, that morale was high and discipline maintained. The general only failed to notice one thing. They were going in the wrong direction.

Much effort has been put into road safety. Mini-roundabouts, sleeping policemen, cats' eyes, white lines, speed traps and cameras. Regulations abound but people still drive too quickly, because in their well-made cars a mere 30 m.p.h. seems so slow, and they feel safe at 50 m.p.h. Perhaps if they felt less safe they would slow down? An experiment which removed cat's eyes and white lines made roads look more dangerous and reduced overall speed as drivers took more responsibility for their own safety. What politician would have the reckless courage to suggest making cars seem less safe to make driving safer? But what kind of bad manager would assume that more rules and safety devices are the only options to consider? Sometimes we are blinded by the glare of our own assumptions. We think within a very limited framework and call it 'realism'. Do meetings keep people informed and accountable? Do they provide collective decisions? Or would it be better to cancel most of them, use email for real emergencies and then catch up with occasional days out at the seaside? When you were handed the problem, did you also inherit a set of limitations to any solution that where not actually necessary?

The chief cause of problems is solutions - Eric Sevareid

3) Decide how best to implement the preferred option

Any action taken by a manager will bring about change. That may just mean bringing an employee up short so they get back to doing what they should have been achieving all along but have been failing to achieve for some time – a return to the *status quo ante*. It may be a new direction or method. In either event, managing change is still a matter of internalising your aims. Some obvious rules would include:

> Your vision of how things ought to be has to be public knowledge – it justifies everything else.
>
> It needs to be heard as your vision – not something imposed upon you by a more senior figure that you are merely tolerating.
>
> The logic behind your vision needs to be explained in simple terms rather than grandiose generalities.
>
> It needs to be clear not only what is wrong with the present but exactly how things will look in the future.
>
> It needs to be clear what time scales apply to that upward journey, and how flexible or unpredictable they may be. Missing deadlines is the best way to reduce commitment; implementing a system before it is ready is also a good way.

It needs to be clear what that depends on and how progress will be evaluated. This is especially true if you are running a pilot. You might be able to run it successfully in the most receptive area of the organisation, and that may be the best way to start, but will it transfer to the least receptive area?

It needs to be clear what it will cost each individual and why that cost is justified.

Involve the pace setters and charismatic leaders as quickly as possible, so they can bring the others.

Find ways to involve everyone, however junior or tangential, so they feel they are consulted. Then they can buy in and may find new solutions precisely because they were not intimately involved in the original idea.

On the other hand, if you can't persuade everyone, don't waste time expecting perfection. If it has to be done, get started.

4) Take necessary actions in good time

This is partly a matter of making decisions clearly and in good time to implement them. But it is also a matter of moving the problem on through the system, which means asserting yourself. Assertion is not aggression. It tends to be weak people who shout and bully. The others speak softly, although they will also carry a big stick. Using it has to be seen as a real option, but only of last resort. The essence of assertiveness is honesty. Staff will be informed of the facts, within any limitations imposed by confidentiality. They will know how you think and why you think it. They will know that you mean what you say and say what you mean. They will have confidence that if a problem occurs you will manage it, not try to avoid or ignore it.

Under those circumstances, you have both the right and the duty to act firmly, to take control.

This may include a habit of congratulating those who deserve it, even seeking out opportunities to do so for relatively small steps. If your public statements are all negative, they can easily be ignored as the ranting of Mr. Grumpy or Ms. Ungrateful. If the problem is structural or procedural then you will need to explain the benefits of the new structure or procedure and allow for the fact that some people will feel attached to it because it is familiar or easy or accords them status or satisfactions that need to be replicated (if deserved and appropriate). If the problem was personal then it is necessary to make sure it is clear that you are criticising the behaviour and not the person – condemn the sin but help the sinner to change by making them feel valued. Even in an informal meeting, comments need to be specific and focused on their effects (in this case you did x and y resulted). In a formal meeting, they may need to be formally evidenced, and you may need to provide them with a representative for their own defence. If the evidence were not sufficient you would not be calling the meeting, so it is to be assumed you kept logs and even witness statements.

However difficult or unpleasant the situation or the meeting, it is always to be assumed that managers stay more calm than those they manage. They may need to explain their own position and even make sure that others understand how they feel. This may include 'let down' or 'concerned' or 'embarrassed'. You will probably need to listen to anger from time to time. But the same rule applies to managers and staff as to teachers and students. There is a distance between them that obliges the figure in authority to behave in a professional manner. That means adopting a professional persona and not removing it in public. If students occasionally behave very badly towards a teacher, it is the persona of the teacher who reacts calmly, not the private individual behind the mask who would like to throw a chair at their heads but does not do so.

The calm persona is the ultimate and at times the only defence against other people's unreasonableness. In times of stress, the calm persona of the manager can reassure. It is part of the job spec that justifies the salary. Provided, of course, that it is studied calm and not stupor. Sometimes the facts of a matter should make one angry – angry enough to act to overcome an injustice – but anger at social injustice is of a different order to merely shouting to be heard. You might share the anger (positive value) but not exhibit the temper (weakness).

Another important element of stress management is the proper use of the student disciplinary code. Managing student behaviour in general is discussed in detail in *Teaching in FE* (chapter 5) but three important principles tend to be confused or ignored. The point of a code is to control, modify and defend. These are not the same functions.

Control

Disciplinary codes mean nothing to any student, and do not affect them, until they become exemplified by an act of expression. Codes do not mean what they say, they mean what are seen to do (Becker,1968, chapt 4). Some rules will be ignored because you do nothing about them or penalties are too slight. The seriousness with which any rule is applied may vary by department or by course. But even if penalties were consistent and the expression of the rules exactly as you would want them, the code may still be ineffective when most needed. The prospect of hanging does not deter murder because most murders are committed in a moment of outrage and passion when reason has no sway. The threat of punishment will not always deter violence of disorder because it may be committed when the student has run out of self-control. Hence the need for conciliation to change behaviours.

Organisations have structures which seem to express values and ideas; they tell you about status and what is normal, acceptable or unthinkable. They construct a reality into which members are socialised. If you want to change an individual within it, to alter the way they behave, you need to change the premises of their decision making. There are limits to human rationality and thus to the amount of information used when making decisions People intend to be rational but actually tend to reach for the first available option. (Salaman and Thompson ed 1973 Chapter 4).

This applies to both students and staff, so decisions made about how to behave, or how to respond to other people's behaviour, may be made (a) in the heat of an uncontrolled moment (b) calmly but too easily and without proper analysis (c) according to the apparent rules of the organisation as they appear from examples of who gets away with what. So offences might be (a) misunderstandings encouraged by the way the organisation has worked so far or (b) acts beyond the control of the offender. The first stage of a disciplinary process needs, then, to be conciliation, in which the offence is explained and contextualised and the offender offered a chance to understand exactly what the rules mean and how they can control their own behaviour. They need to change the basis on which they make decisions.

Helping students to behave differently is not a simple or short-term task and is best done by example. Does the organisation behave as you want the student to behave? Is it calm, firm, consistent and fair or does it vacillate and then strike out? Are the human frailties of the staff writ large in the results of the code on students?

It may be that management of the code is delegated and you will only come across the problem when there is an appeal. In that case, it is even more important that the day-to-day operators are trained in consistent application, and that hearings are (a) properly supplied with all evidence in good time (b) conducted calmly but in an efficient time scale (c) decisive.

Defend

Some behaviours will prove impossible to modify sufficiently, or sufficiently quickly, and the offender (student or staff) will have to be removed, either temporarily or permanently, to defend the majority from intolerable pressures. Attempts to conciliate, understand and be sympathetic are not the same as the use of a sympathetic persona to mask indecisiveness. It is common for a violent or even aggressive offender to be suspended until the formal hearing, so that tempers can cool and further offence be avoided. On the same basis, firm action is better than no action. Managers are there to manage, not to try to be popular by being nice to everyone while Rome burns. The meaning of the student code is defined by your actions.

Listening

Hearing is not the same as actively listening – seeking for clues to what is being said, what is meant and the most useful way to respond. "I heard you" can include "but ignored you."

It takes a great deal of self-control to listen without replying, especially if you disagree. But you can't win any argument without understanding what is being said first, and that means holding back.

You need to tell people that you are willing to listen as part of your job and reinforce that by actually doing it regularly. Only repeated examples will convince people that (a) you mean it but (b) listening need not mean agreeing.

It is most efficient to set aside certain times for this process. This reinforces the intention but also limits the time it takes. Regular short meetings for updates are better than emergency sessions when it is too late you don't have head space.

Avoid enforced meetings when you don't have time and are not really listening properly. If it can't wait until the next scheduled time then make an appointment for later. If you have explained the logic of your position in advance this will be understood as efficiency and not rejection. Some managers like to keep an open door policy so staff feel they can come in with problems to be solved, which can lead to the manager not completing the important tasks because of constant interruption. It is occasionally necessary to close the door and focus on strategy, or gain critical distance. On the other hand, a door that is closed too often seems to indicate a manager not coping, or not caring. The balance is to be accessible but not always on demand, to decide what is important and stick to it.

Some people will be personally annoying. They speak stridently, waste time on pettifogging complaints and seem mainly concerned with their own comfort. For as long as they are employees they also need to be heard, if only so you can understand what it must be like for their colleagues, but they may need training in effective presentation and understanding the main issue.

Don't hide behind your desk, come out and sit beside them. Make sure no papers are left around that shouldn't be seen and don't answer the telephone until it is over - you are busy focusing on them. It may sometimes be better, if practical, to visit their space.

Being seen to listen means controlling your body language (impatience and boredom will show). Without being too theatrical, it is worth making the effort to lean forward, nod, maintain eye contact etc. It is important not to interrupt with a 'solution' before they have finished explaining the problem – it is like telling students the answers instead of guiding them to work it out. Or like saying "shut up and go away."

More importantly, try to summarise what was said and repeat it, to make sure you have really understood it. Often, you will have unconsciously changed their emphasis to your own benefit, and will need correcting. It is the elements you didn't hear, or didn't want to hear, that may need most discussion.

As with students, open questions tend to elicit more useful responses than closed questions, although for the nervous they may also seem threatening, a fishing trip for you to trip them up.

Questions can also lead the interlocutor through a more efficient thought process. How's it going? Why is that a problem? How can it be solved? What can we do about it, what do each of us need to contribute?

Running and attending meetings

There are two types of meeting you might a run, a one-to-one and a more general committee style.

The one-to-one meeting (or hosting a small number of visitors) needs listening skills mentioned above, but additionally note the following:

If you are the host you control the space. You can position the visitor anywhere you like and side-by-side with a writing space within reach will look more friendly, and thus more confident, than anything that resembles a barricade.

If you permit interruptions you not only lose track of the discussion but also imply the discussion is not sufficiently important, which alienates your visitor.

If you don't allow adequate time, you will not cover the ground properly and give the impression you are not taking it seriously. If you allow too much time, then, as the Peter Principle warns, work will grow to fill the space allotted to it.

You need to be very clear before you start what you hope to achieve from that meeting, who and how. You need to imagine what success would look like – what would enable you to state that objectives were met and the meeting over, **but**

You also need to be capable of realising when new information or ideas may demand a change of direction. That is not the same as being sidetracked.

You need to state the purpose of the meeting clearly and make sure your visitor has identical notions of purpose. If their objectives are different that may be the purpose for the meeting to reach a compromise, but that needs to be made explicit.

At the end of the meeting, you should be able to agree what has been agreed and who will do what as a result. This needs to be written down and given to all parties. With internal visitors you can give them notes made during the meeting and photocopied. With external visits you may wish to consider the wording before mailing notes later.

Management by busyness

Mr. X was formally responsible for a major project but delegated responsibility to two managers. They asked to speak with him about a number of issues that concerned them. One issue needed his formal agreement to implement a decision. His PA booked them an appointment then later cancelled it. Under persuasion, she found another time, but had some difficulty doing so – "he is very busy, you know".

When they arrived, he was dealing with his emails and asked them to wait until he finished a reply. They finally started the discussion and, as decisions were being taken, his PA put through a 'phone call from an outside agency. He took the call and decided he had to consult another person about it.

Disappearing to do so, he left his two visitors in his office. He finally returned to stress that the project in question was "very important" and had to succeed. Before he could agree to their proposal he needed to consult, but he promised a decision soon. He returned to his email system to write a note about the 'phone call he had just taken.

For external visitors it is particularly important to

> be ready on time (too long in reception implies lack of consideration, lack of efficiency and lack of authority)

be aware of any personal needs they may have (refreshments, toilets etc.) and begin with the usual opening pleasantries about their health or journey, but without wasting time on a long debate concerning the state of the motorways in the UK - get on with the job and let them go again.

Committees are a different matter.

> A committee is a cul-de-sac down which ideas are lured and then quietly strangled. - Sir Barnett Cocks

Everyone attends meetings and everyone complains there are too many, too long and too pointless. So why do we hold them? Health and Safety is the flavour of the month so there is an H&S committee. It is then placed on the agenda of departmental meetings so the H&S rep can report back. The H&S rep is allotted time, which is always filled because 'work expands to fill the time allotted to it'. Meetings never finish early, however small the amount of important content. The minutes are stored to be shown to inspectors, who know how little they are worth and spend more time listening to students and staff to see if the meeting made any difference to their experience.

Of course, you need to consult and inform people. Of course, you need to record actions as evidence. But are large meetings the best way to do that, and are words really evidence of activity? You might consider a system that insists:

1) If it is only information being **passed on**, it can be loaded to the intranet and a short (very short) summary circulated without comment.

2) If the information needs to be **explained** then a time limit of five minutes can be imposed.

3) If the information needs to be **discussed** then a time limit of ten minutes can be imposed.

4) If a **conclusion** has to be reached then consensus is preferred, but it is a matter of judgement whether more time would provide it more readily than firm leadership from someone who took the trouble to think through the information beforehand (under urgent/important).

5) If **action** is to be taken then it is to be taken. The agenda should automatically record the action point and hold someone **accountable**. If action is not taken by the next meeting, then a failure to act needs to be explained and recorded. There are few experiences more corrosive to any teacher or manager than sitting through a meeting where colleagues have failed to act on an item without any penalties being attached to that failure. Why bother to have meetings if it is all words and no action?

The agenda should make it clear what is expected by what time. It can be flexible, but not vacuous.

Of course, there is more to social interaction than exchanging terse action points. Personalities interact, bonds are formed, emotional reactions take place. The affective is as much a part of any teaching as the cognitive, and the same is true of some meetings. The standard of refreshment can make a bigger difference to any outcome than the arguments in any briefing paper. But if there is no real outcome, think of all the useful things you could have been doing instead. Life is too short, education too fundamental a matter, to be wasting time just sitting about feeling important at a big polished table.

Often, the real power of a meeting lies not in the chair but in the writing of minutes. It is with reference to those minutes that permissions are granted or withheld, and their phrasing can be crucial. Sometimes, as an act of managerial cowardice, comments made in the meeting are shaded differently when written up. If your organisation has not been trained in the use of Plain English, the time may be wasted interpreting or arguing over obscure sentences. Both problems can be avoided by signalling the end of debate by reading into the minutes a sentence that is taken by the chair to reflect what the meeting wished to be recorded. It is often argued the real power lies with the chair's PA, because the PA writes the minutes and by the time the chair reads them no-one can recall what was said, so only the PA version has any currency. It is better practice to read, approve and send them out quickly, so that anyone required to take action is reminded to do so in good time. If they only ever arrive with the agenda for the next meeting, it is too late to be of any use and this encourages the view that paperwork is without any reference to reality.

Negotiating

Whether in committee, formal or informal meetings, you will at some point need to negotiate your way to the desired outcome. Negotiations tend to be quicker and more successful if you can:

Be clear before you start what you hope to gain and why; what you need to avoid and why.

Be prepared to explain that to the other side.

Know which points of your argument they are most likely to criticise or reject, and why.

Be clear what you can afford to lose or give in order to reach compromise.

Before you meet, imagine an outcome that would enable both sides to feel they have gained.

See the other person's point of view and be prepared to help them to get what they want – they may not be good negotiators. Even if they are, rapport saves time.

Remember the rules of good listening and use questions as much as statements.

Treat negative responses as valid points of view, but also as stages in the process.

As with students, rather than criticising their arguments and fighting for dominance, provide them with ideas and helpful comments that will allow them to discover their own errors, and a way to back down without losing face.

At the end of the session, record a form of words you can agree on, even if it is only a friendly way to express the sticking points at this stage.

Power in human relations is rare; influence is more common and often more useful. Positional authority is less useful than the influence of a good reputation and influence can work upwards and sideways whereas authority cannot.

5) Check on the result

Whatever actions you bring about, however right you think you were to achieve change, as nobody is perfect you have to be sure that the effects are what you intended. All new ideas have potentially unforeseen consequences that may need accounting for. An impact assessment might be carried out before and after any major event/decision.

6) Ask what you can learn from the experience admit mistakes

If the results are not what you hoped for, you will need to go back and admit your errors. Everyone knows that mangers are imperfect. Only the worst managers fail to remember that or refuse to admit it. If things go badly wrong, then pressure may turn to stress. That is not always avoidable.

The best way to deal with stress is to avoid it. It is worth re-reading the advice above to see if you can work your way back to mere pressure. If not, then it is some comfort to recall that work-related stress is widespread. Keele University looked at the primary and secondary sectors with a survey of 688 Heads. Their report[20] claimed over 25% were so stressed their job affected their relationship and 10% claimed it played a part in breaking up that relationship. Heads admitted to examples of excluding or wrongly placing students, missing out on funds and mistreating staff through tiredness. Meanwhile, one in five children in schools lose sleep worrying about SATs, bullying and workloads.

There is something badly wrong with either the way we choose Heads, the way we train them or, more likely, the way the education system adopted punitive modes of behaviour under the mistaken impression that waving a big stick somehow, on its own, made people more efficient – an ignorant error unworthy of the educated. There is now a shortage of applicants for Headships. Teacher Support Network receives calls from teachers in colleges and Universities, 3% of which are about bullying and heavy workloads. Their blog[21] was set up to combat bullying.

In industry as a whole, occupational physicians are seeing three times the number of people with stress. It is unlikely that is all due just to an increased tendency to seek help or admit problems. The Rising Sun Anger Bar in Nanjing was set up in April 2006 to offer a valuable service to Chinese workers. It contains large men in body armour and for a modest fee you can beat them mercilessly. Stress and unreleased anger are fatal elements of industrial and commercial development.

In such a context, telling people to breathe deeply and cling on is not responsible behaviour. Stress that continues has to be

---

[20] TES 5th May 2006

[21] www.bulliedacademics.blogspot.com

removed by taking action. Standing in the rain with an umbrella is not as useful as moving indoors. However, if stress is a short term penalty with the prospect of change, then ways to cope with it include the following.

Find in your lists of urgent/important tasks something you can finish and break it into smaller stages so you can finish them and tick them off. If you find you are spending time worrying about work or complaining about stress, stop and get back to finishing that small task.

But also take breaks. Working until you are tired means working inefficiently. You spend longer and longer achieving less and less. Covering a page with words you later have to erase is less useful than taking a walk outside, after which you may find you have a more succinct version ready in your head.

It is not a break if you just go to the canteen and somehow in the process get stopped, delayed and lumbered with another problem. But, if you are in control, then a change of task or even a change of environment may still refresh.

Some people find it useful to repeat a phrase with a calming or rhythmic effect, or to visualise a favourite scene. Others don't, and a sticky bun or a good Chablis has more effect. Calories feed the brain, so don't miss lunch. Spoil yourself if you can. But, at the same time, remember that exercise not only tones the machine you live in, but also works off aggression. Consider the incidence of heart attacks. Anger kills but exercise saves lives.

Breaks also means holidays. Some people find taking a holiday stressful in itself. It is not uncommon to hear a manager say they didn't have time to take their whole allocation. It is sometimes more effective to take your breaks in short doses but more often – a series of long weekends. But take them all. You may achieve more at work if you are there less often, but more rested when you arrive.

Recalling the advice above under 'listening'. Manage interruptions and, if you have an important/urgent task, do it now. Small steps better than no steps. Think of yourself as a student frightened by homework. How would you advise them?

And if you have expressed your irritation or stress in an email, don't send it. Read it again in the morning, and ask if you really want it to represent you in public. If things need to be said, then make sure you say them, in a format carefully considered. Don't get mad, get even.

Ask yourself, if you could have whatever you wanted, what would success look like? If you had to make do with present limitations, what would success look like then? Imagining it may be the first step to achieving it.

If none of that works, and you are losing sleep, maybe you would be better elsewhere?

> You decide where you're going and you bloody well get there. Don't talk about it, do it.
>
> Trudy Norris-Grey,
> UK President Sun Microsystems
> *Observer Business Section,* September 2006

Chapter 5

Curriculum design and finance

> The recommendations of this Review are the product
> of extensive discussions and represent an agreed path to
> an improved future, a path guided by principles we can
> all share. In certain cases, individuals and employers are
> supposed to be contributing alongside Government to
> the costs of Further Education courses, on account of
> the benefits they derive from them. In this report, I
> have called this 'co-investment'. The current system for
> ensuring this co-investment happens is not fit for
> purpose.   BIS 2010

Or, to put it in simple terms, get lost. Government won't
pay for what the skilled bodies it claims to want so you'll have
to get it from students or employers. It is no surprise that funds
are dying up even as demands increase, but that what do
financial pressures imply for curriculum design?

Managers often feel their main task is to account for
expense and maximise income. The job is then complicated by
'firefighting', dealing with the many small problems that arise
from day to day and prevent strategic planning. Difficult people
get in the way of the 'main task'. Still other people demand
figures and plans, impose accountabilities and expect reports.
Somewhere in the muddle, somebody has to work out who
should be learning what, how, why and when. Obviously, that is
your main purpose. Anything that detracts from it is secondary.
Your key output is a successful student, not a series of reports
about them.

New courses or changes in curriculum design might arise
from exterior pressures, national initiatives or an internal
suggestion with special pleading (I want to run this course, can
I have permission?). In deciding what is important and urgent,
prior to making an action plan for the day, week or year, it is

useful to clarify the basic principles that inform the purpose of FE according to its major funding body. One version of a manager's function used to be protecting the organisation from it paymasters:

> Colleges tried to maximise funding while the FEFC scrutinised and inspected. Hence the perception in colleges that bureaucracy derived from mistrust: to a large extent it did. - LSC (2002) p18

In the early days of the new reform movement, one of the more unfortunate attempts to make providers more accountable for the fate of their students was the notion of unit funding. Rather than hand over a lump sum, the funds were apportioned for outcomes, with some set aside for initial advice, guidance and induction, some for teaching term by term and a proportion for final success. There were many unintended outcomes. Cash flow was unpredictable. Risk-taking became an expensive gamble. Disciplinary hearings tended to keep one eye on the termly cut-off dates, so that troublesome students were retained until after the funding deadline for that term. Skillful manipulators found that changes in the programme design could put students through a different set of qualifications and thus increase the unit funding without significantly altering their learning experience. Management was about playing the game by looking for loopholes. Even when the worst excesses were removed by abolishing that system, there remained the problem of planning by rules and targets that produced ironic results:

> The allocation system produced perverse outcomes in that it encouraged colleges to maximise their bids for growth funds, irrespective of whether they were realistic or not and then to delay the final reconciliation as long as possible – the only financial outcome of reconciliation being clawback as there was no additional funding for extra activity. Hence there was, year-on-

year, a systematic underachievement against targets.

LSC (2002) p19

> You can trade-off success rate against numbers. If you're over recruiting and the LSC are not paying for these, there is the opportunity to reclassify this as additional non-LSC funding provision which takes this out of the success rates calculation. You can also look at the system and look at splitting courses. If you subdivided long courses and create short courses from these you can reduce the dropout rates. So, for example, rather than having a 33 week long, part-time maths course, you can split it into a 10-week foundation course, and then a further 23 week course with the qualification being linked to this final element.

Principal cited in Smith and Bailey (2006) p 10

Constant tinkering with the system was forced by a funding process whose complexity remained counter-productive, but one by-product in the example cited above might have been useful in terms of motivation. But a low hurdle to achieve early success followed by a separate hurdle once students feel confident might have been a good idea for quite different reasons. A rise in success rates is the major aim, and ought not to be only the by-product of the manipulation of regulations.

Now that funding is plan-led, the atmosphere in which planning takes place is intended to be different. Instead of a narrow focus on counting heads and classifying them according to financial value, the starting point is an agreement as to the purpose of the provider in local and national terms, a contract to carry out a social and political purpose to certain agreed standards. Depending on the level at which you operate in your present role, you may have more or less direct influence on the negotiations with funding bodies, although you ought to have a proportionate influence on those who do the negotiating. Responding to national agendas is part of the process, but so is a sensitive analysis of data in which any provider who knows their market can argue their case. The 'partnership' is more likely to be equal if it is clear that arguments are evidence-based and an argument based on clear principles of social value is more likely to be effective. Therefore, future, curriculum design should be about success rates, but not in the narrow and outmoded sense of manipulating outcomes by playing with regulations.

There is a larger, more mature and more imaginative kind of thinking behind the more recent language used in discussing funding and targets, although questions were still being begged. The first priority is still raising the level 2 achievement at 19, which is obviously going to be easier if the GCSE system if revised or replaced and school students are offered a better range of certification systems, encouraging more suitable learning experiences. The funding gap between FE and schools is reduced but adult learning has been subject to "a tighter focus on key priorities ... involving more provision delivered at full cost and a significant increase in fees, but with a safeguarded level of public funding for Personal and Community Development Learning". Emphasis continues to be on "funding vocational learning that is valued by employers, with colleges and providers developing close employer links that inform the curriculum".

> The most important aspect of this approach is a step change in rebalancing public and private contributions to the cost of learning.   LSC (2005) 13 & 14

So there are financial constraints on the freedom of any prospective students to access a learning opportunity:

> The long term aim for employers and learners to contribute more to the cost of their training will require colleges to be more commercially astute. Increasing fee

income is a significant challenge for colleges. Colleges will need to develop business plans including reshaping their programmes to offer more courses for which people are prepared to pay, and to target their Learner Support Funds to mitigate the effects of fee increases on people less able to pay. CPA (2006)

On the other hand, the white paper argued

Alongside the core economic mission, we remain strongly committed to learning for personal fulfilment, civic participation and community development, and are taking steps to strengthen the range and quality of such provision. We have allocated £210 million in 2006-07 for personal and community development learning (PCDL), and we will maintain this level of funding in 2007-08. But there will increasingly be an expectation that individuals should pay for this kind of provision where they can afford to do so. DfES (2006) 2.45

So the skill of the senior manager is to persuade the funding bodies which social, economic and political aims are justified and agree funded targets for meeting them. This will be easier if they have partners from the local community to speak with them. The skill of the middle manager is to find ways to reach those potential learners who have been accepted as valid concerns. This will be easier of they have partners in the local community to advise them. Depending on the size of the provider and the way management is conducted, there will be more or less interchange between those tasks and personnel, but what counts as a reasonable target, both for cohorts and success rates, will depend partly on what kind of curriculum design process has been employed or envisaged. Partners may be brought on board in many different ways.

A good example of the inseparability of funding and c.d. models was the growth of effective partnerships to manage 14-16 links under Increased Flexibility (IF) a programme arising out of the White Paper, *Schools: Achieving Success* (July 2001.)

Research had clearly established that in real terms colleges subsidise the students sent to them by schools:

> The college subsidy is between 45% and 66%, depending on the overhead rate used. Of even more significance, the table shows that schools and LEAs as only contributing between 20% and 30% of the total costs of provision provided for their pupils.
>
> Styles and Fletcher (2006) p14

There were large variations in the way colleges worked out their overheads and even larger variations in the charges they made to schools, but there was also a tendency to carry the cost because it was worth the investment to improve relationships with local schools and, ultimately, to improve recruitment (ibid).

Behind that argument there were others about the effect and value of the 14-16 presence. Before IF arrived many providers were involved with Work-Related Learning (WRL). A common model was for schools to send to local colleges those students who were not succeeding on academic courses but might perhaps re-engage on vocational programmes. This often meant cohorts with learning difficulties and behavioural problems, and schools would pay external providers for the service at a price to be agreed locally. Curricula were designed with learning difficulties and behavioural problems in mind – they were short, practical and had low hurdles they could clear early to increase confidence.

When IF started it was supposed to increase the status of vocational education by attracting students with more potential to take vocational GCSEs, but only a portion of the cohort were obliged to take them and there was no immediate move to clawback funds if outcomes were below the expected minimum. The way in which schools responded to this opportunity varied widely, as did restrictions placed upon entry by providers.

Some schemes were small and selective. They were restricted

to students with particularly good records in attendance and achievement in school. Other providers used this opportunity to take in larger numbers of the students who had previously wanted to come on WRL links but were denied for lack of funds. Some students were interviewed and selected with careful reference to personal career aims, others were shovelled in to courses with scant regard for their preference.

Even those who had not particularly wanted to attend sometimes responded to the new environment positively in the sense that they found they preferred it, but enjoying the environment did not always equate to succeeding academically or in career aims. The aims of the funding bodies, providers, school and students were far from coherent. There was not always a serious attempt to relate IF work outside to work carried out in school, so that the two curricula were not always seen as relevant to each other by those taking them or even, in any detail, by those managing them. Qualifications might be the subject of trading between schools and providers, matching spare capacity to demand without relevance to labour market needs or future progression opportunities. Providers might use IF as a marketing tool or income stream [22] and schools as a short-term solution to disaffection.

There were also many positive elements of the IF process (sources for both positive and negative evidence are referenced below) but it is worth stressing the muddle that attended some provision because so much of it was finance-based. Schools had to pay for WRL. In most cases, IF places were subsidised. Although the costings used in allocating places varied widely [23], IF was financially more attractive to a school than WRL. Some therefore saw IF as a means of getting more WRL places under another name, and had no reason to explore new curriculum models beyond asking what they could get for free in

[22] Seven out of the 30 partnerships include colleges that charged for delivery, generating between £12k and £80k of additional funding (ibid)
[23] The average charge per student was £513 over two years. The highest charge of £1,200 per student worked out as £300 per student per day. - LSC IF costing study final report - December 2003

vocational areas popular with low achievers. Partnerships that should have been used for positive planning remained only as trading rings.

One possible solution to this was also finance led. In area X, IF funds were provided as a lump sum. The numbers of places to be provided for this sum varied widely from a national minimum, so colleges had some discretion. There was also some discretion in charges made for materials, transport etc. Courses lasted for one day and were seen as a marketing tool.

WRL places were charged for at a rate fixed by agreement, with some LEA or LSC pressure to keep it 'reasonable'. Courses usually lasted for half a day, with a potential extension at extra cost. They were seen as a service, either social or commercial depending on who you asked in the college.

Schools considered the WRL price to be high and some wanted to use IF places to extend provision. The means by which students were selected by schools varied in quality and integrity. As the number of WRL-type students increased, so did the need for LSAs and other support and thus real costs.

It was decided to offer only one set of options across the board, abolishing the titles WRL and IF. Some would be for a day and some for half a day. Some would be level 2 and some level 1. The provider would go to the school and discus these with all students and parents who were interested, then invite students in for a day's practical experience and a screening test. Final allocations would be negotiated with the schools on the basis of all available evidence, with support needs discussed at the time. The idea of competing for places on the day made them seem more valuable and rewarded effort in workshops as much as any academic record, but also put a premium on behaviour during a critical period.

The cost for any course, whether a day or half a day, would be the same. The figure would be calculated by looking at the previous year's income and adding the usual WRL income to the usual IF income, then dividing it by the usual combined number of students it covered. This provided an average that spread IF subsidy and school costs across the board. Schools who had been paying WRL fees as well and obtaining free IF places were not significantly affected financially – it evened out – but in future all decision about curriculum and placement were taken for educational reasons, not financial reasons. Students with most potential and suitable behaviour received more hours and higher level courses – others received a platform from which they could prove themselves worthy of promotion if they wished. Schools were also invited to provide their own vocational options and trade places instead of paying charges.

The major result of this change in funding was not financial but cultural. Once the fee was fixed – an annual event - providers and schools could ask teachers to talk about individual places without worrying that a decision about curriculum choice had immediate financial consequences. Tensions based on financial consequences were passed up the line and debate was not about what a service would cost but whether student A could benefit more or less than student B. The fact that some of the provision was always the half-day level 1 model meant that the college could not just accept the best academically for its own benefit – it would always take a proportion of the less able, which reassured school planners.

So, funding decisions might clear the ground, force the issue or free up the thinking process or curriculum design. But what are the issues when designing curricula? The LSDA ran an interesting project to explore how to "develop a curriculum for excellence" (Hughes at al 2004) [24] and the initial focus of the report was not on changing it radically but enhancing and improving it. They give several examples of how standards were raised within the course by exposing students to the experience of high standards elsewhere (p22) and perhaps the

---

[24] "Excellence" is one of the words listed by Best (2006) and will continue to annoy in some of its applications. It is true that in any group the majority will be average; that is what 'average' means. But it is also true that the average can usually be higher. It might be more useful if, instead of aiming for 'excellence' we were aiming for excitement, or pride.

most important element of the much mentioned concept of 'excellence' is that it cannot be taught without being modelled. Students may have experienced the sloppy and second rate for so long they cannot imagine what real quality feels like, and need to be inspired by it. The idea of high standards needs, in Keatsian terms, to be 'proved upon the pulse'. That is one of many reasons why mentors are useful. To observe someone similar to them achieving something obviously impressive helps them to feel that competence is within reach. To act as a mentor gives students a sense of achievement and confidence. Hughes et al mention demonstrations as another way to raise pride in achievement (p25) and thus, eventually, standards. Neither idea is expensive or difficult.

When the curriculum does need changing, it need not mean totally re-writing the whole programme. Hughes et al (2004) cite examples where adding further elements can increase breadth (27) and master classes changed the relationship between students and tutors. Some colleges opened libraries for longer or at weekends (29). The combination of measures increased "confidence, professionalism and self-esteem" (p33), gave excellent attendance and punctuality (p35) and involved learners in actively planning their own futures. One interesting lesson was that NVQs, which do not distinguish between pass, merit and distinction, need to be supplemented by something that does (p51). Why try to be excellent when scraping through yields the same result? Sometimes a curriculum just needs a more encouraging grading system, a reason to try harder. And, of course, the involvement of employers was an important element (see chapter 7). They show convincingly that

> Implementing a curriculum to support excellence does not call for rocket science and does not cost the earth - (p1)

Sometimes, however, programmes might need to be redesigned, or at least audited to check their suitability and efficiency, and when they are it is necessary to have a model to work from. These are key questions to address when creating or reforming a curriculum:

> Does it reflect national and local priorities as firmly established in your approved plan?

> If so, what data from the SAR underpinned the agreement and if not what data would persuade them to adopt it?

> Does this data provide evidence and rationale that clearly shows:

> A need for the skills you wish to develop?

> Progression routes into HE and/or work?

> A gap in the market (a real need for more provision, or for a new kind?)

> That this form of provision is the most effective and equitable (f/t or p/t? modular? Distance or e-learning? Flexible hours?). Are any potential applicants excluded or discouraged by your model?

In looking at resource and staffing implications, have you taken account of the resources and staffing of all actual and potential partners in the area?

What is known about the learning preferences of the most likely applicants/previous or typical students? How does the curriculum model address potential teaching and learning issues in this vocational area at this level? Has any research affected your thinking here?

> What input have interested parties been able to make to the planning process, at what stage? Would this include

schools, careers adviser, employers (locally and/or through SSCs), unions?

Are the learning and programme outcomes couched in language and set at levels clearly and realistically related to the potential progression routes (in other words do you have proof they need to know precisely these things and not more or different things?)

What skills, experience and knowledge do you really need to succeed in this programme? How are they best demonstrated by potential applicants?

Are the methods of assessment and certification suitable for the potential cohorts? For example, do you need graded outcomes to differentiate and does it really have to be a written test?

What can you say about the integration of instrumental skills that would show they are (a) encouraged by the curriculum (b) at a suitable standard for progression?

What kinds of support or enhancements might be required to achieve excellent results and are those habits and costings built in to the standard model, or have you left excellence as an option?

Inspectors now want to see evidence of self-analysis and self-regulation. It would be useful to apply such analysis to existing provision as part of the SAR process, but slowly and one course at a time, so that responses lead to remedial action and not to the sense of being overwhelmed.

Chapter 6

Equal Opportunities

The new framework for Ofsted inspection has a much stronger focus on equal opportunities, with significantly greater scrutiny of equality progress and practice. In addition, the inspection grade for equal opportunities is a limiting grade, for the first time. The grade will contribute to, and may limit inspection grades for leadership and management, and overall effectiveness. For example, if a judgment of inadequate is made for equal opportunities, then the provider will not get better than satisfactory for overall effectiveness, and it is likely that the grade for this will be inadequate. If a college is judged to be satisfactory for equal opportunities, then it is unlikely that overall effectiveness will be better than good.

Equality, Diversity and Governance;
Brief Guide for governors and clerks in further education colleges,
Christine Rose, LSIS 2009

The FE system must be the powerhouse for delivering the skills at all levels that are needed to sustain an advanced, competitive economy and make us a fairer society, offering equal opportunities for all based on talent and effort, not background. DfES (2006) E.S. 3

Issues of inequality are also of particular importance in the post-16 education sector where FE organisations operate at the 'leading edge' of poverty and disadvantage in their local communities. .... Colleges play a valuable, but often under-valued role in trying to ameliorate disadvantage and one of its most difficult associated effects: disengaged and ill-disciplined students. Issues of deprivation, poverty and inequality constitute an enormous leadership challenge for those in post-16 education. Colleges frequently 'inherit' many deep-seated community-based social and economic problems that are very difficult to change in any fundamental sense.... While these issues of disadvantage within the sector focus most directly upon the FE colleges, they also increasingly impact on 6th Form Centres. Collinson (2006) pp13-14

Here are some questions you have probably thought about already:

What sort of equality is possible in a college?

What aspects of a college might be dysfunctional and/or manageable in this context?

How do you prioritise and monitor progress?

What is 'reasonable behaviour', in legal and in policy terms?

I did not begin by referring to the Equality Act. Any conversation that starts by asking about your legal obligations is in danger of becoming defensive and worrying to much about protecting your own back and interpreting the letter of the law. In fact, the only way to be sure you are acting reasonably (= defensibly) is to understand the spirit of the law and apply it as a matter of principle. There is a crucial difference between passive 'management' and active 'leadership'.

passive 'management'	active leadership
Focus on the letter of the law.	Understand the spirit of the law.
Publish policies and documents.	Proceed by conversations/consultation to evolve policy.

Push responsibility down the chain by making sure all staff have signed up to 'training' so they are legally assumed to have read the policy...	Embed good practice and ensure feedback loops to check policies are implemented and effective.
Assume that if nobody complains the policies work.	Interrogate data and carry out impact assessments to ensure there is no problem undiscovered/unrecognised.
Focus on defending those in authority against complaints and attacks. Risk alienating staff by defending the institution	Focus on helping those in need by applying authority to social issues. Accept that the learning community needs to act from a sense of common purpose and values.
Result not legally acceptable as 'reasonable steps'	Result ensures that reasonable steps are taken routinely.

Bearing that in mind, it is now worth stating that the Equality Act 2010[25] contains an Equality Duty to

> eliminate unlawful discrimination, harassment and victimisation and any other conduct prohibited by the Act

> advance equality of opportunity between people who share a protected characteristic and people who do not share it

---

[25] http://www.legislation.gov.uk/ukpga/2010/15/contents

> foster good relations between people who share a
> protected characteristic and people who do not share it

The public sector Equality Duty at section 149 requires public bodies to consider all individuals when carrying out their day-to-day work; in shaping policy, in delivering services and in relation to their own employees. It requires public bodies to have due regard to the need to

> eliminate discrimination
>
> advance equality of opportunity
>
> and foster good relations between different people when carrying out their activities.

The Equality Duty supports good decision making – it encourages public bodies to understand how different people will be affected by their activities, so that their policies and services are appropriate and accessible to all and meet different people's needs. By understanding the effect of their activities on different people, and how inclusive public services can support and open up people's opportunities, public bodies can be more efficient and effective. The Equality Duty therefore helps public bodies to deliver the Government's overall objectives for public services.

The Act refers to 'public bodies'. Although colleges are not now be classed as public bodies for financial purposes, it is unlikely that will make any difference to obligations under the Act, as it is also clear the regulations apply to anyone in a strategic or funding relationship with a public body[26].

If you have any questions about any of the terms it uses you will find all its terms defined in Schedule 28. But first consider these key terms in layman's language:

---

[26] see section 1 and a legal judgement referred to in
http://archive.leadermagazine.co.uk/article.php?id=791

Equality is a question of removing obstacles so that nobody is disadvantaged as they try to gain an education or employment. Obstacles might be physical, economic, cultural, sociological or psychological. It is a matter of acting fairly. It does not mean equality of outcome or of treatment but of opportunity and value.

Diversity is a question of treating people with respect and consideration, ensuring that all members of society are treated as an equal part of that society and feel equally valued in the learning or working environment. It is a matter of acting in a civilised, well-mannered way. It is not a matter of somehow 'forcing' the college to reflect the diversity of the community in strictly % terms, but of asking why it does not and drawing conclusions which are acted on.

To deny either is to act in a way that runs contrary to our best values as a country / society and is essentially uneducated behaviour. To fail in either is also bad business. The terms apply to both staff and students and the right approach enables you to draw from a wider pool of talent and maximise achievement.

Inclusive practice means teaching/managing in such a way that you have planned to allow for known or likely differences and done what might reasonably be expected of you to allow everyone to benefit to the best of their ability. There is always debate on whether inclusion is always the best practice for some students in mainstream schools but that is not related to the problem of making it harder for some groups to learn by not thinking through how you organise the system and the venue then organise and present your ideas.

Community includes both the local community - who are not always integrated or cohesive - and the international business clients. Note in FE the unique experience of forcing a wide range of people into a small area – a social microcosm causing stresses not experienced elsewhere, so that pressures and frictions are likely to be disproportionally high.

Ofsted now assumes that appropriate values will underpin all actions will in future report on equality and diversity under the three key headlines of: outcomes for learners; teaching, learning and assessment; and leadership and management. Equality is not a kind of bolt-on or appendix but a fundamental aspect of the educational system and their intention is to "place greater emphasis on the impact for learners and reduce the focus on policies and procedures". In other works – it is not what you say that counts but you behave, and how students feel. And providers are supposed to be proactive, showing how they interrogate data to look for problems and solve them, then go back to evaluate the effects of their action plans. The focus is less on writing and filing than on action and effects. Your impact assessment counts far more than your printed intentions or policies. Action plans are to be acted on - one aim that is pursued through an impact assessment is better than four that sound good but have little effect.

Interestingly, the Act refers to protected characteristics covered by the Equality Duty:

age

disability

gender reassignment

marriage and civil partnership (but only in respect of eliminating unlawful discrimination)

pregnancy and maternity

race – this includes ethnic or national origins, colour or nationality

religion or belief – this includes lack of belief

sex

sexual orientation

But protected characteristics do not include lack on income or savings, family poverty, family tradition of being NEET etc, although the opening of the Act includes the basic idea that relevant bodies must:

> when making decisions of a strategic nature about how to exercise its functions, have due regard to the desirability of exercising them in a way that is designed to reduce the inequalities of outcome which result from socio-economic disadvantage - 1.1.(1).

Of course, there are other factors (e.g. funding agency priorities) that would persuade us to include lack of income, so that the local Index of Multiple Deprivation (IMD) is also part of the planning.

> The gap between the best and worst performers in our system actually widens as they go through education; and it is both significantly wider and more closely related to socio-economic status in this country than elsewhere - DfES (2004) Chapt. 1 para 23

The census offers data by various categories or areas which are explained on their site. They include:

Local Authority
Ward
New Deal For Communities
Output Area
Lower Layer Super Output Area
Middle Layer Super Output Area
Primary Care Organisation
Health Authority
Education Authority
Westminster Parliamentary Constituency
Parish

Local information from other sources may be more recent,

perhaps a survey carried out by the local authority on a particular area or aspect of deprivation, and an annual survey of the percentage of free school dinners provided in each school. However, the IMD will be a useful indicator for most purposes, including analysis of where most social need occurs or backing a claim for funding to tackle it.

There may be some fiddling at the edges. IMDs are provided by wards any weighting for Additional Social Need may be fixed by postcode. But experienced MIS with a good map will be able to provide enough data for any manager to know with reasonable certainty the socio-economic climate surrounding an applicant, if not, of course, the personal circumstances. The latter may vary considerably within the former. Area A may contain two estates that seem similar to any outsider, but there is likely to be a whole series of small differences between them that are vital to their members, and fierce tribal loyalties will maintain that difference. Nevertheless, it is useful at times to remind staff within the organisation of the makeup of any community in which they live and work. Are they aware how many people in ward x have no inside toilet or are likely to have several generations unemployed? How high and how ghettoed the incidences of single-parentage or disengagement from post-16 education or young carers? How has this affected primary and secondary schools and thus the point scores and career aims of applicants?

Also, single characteristics may, in real life, merge confusingly. When is a problem identified as 'ethnic minority' actually one of social class/housing/MID etc.? If all recent immigrants happen to be crowded into an area with poorer housing and higher unemployment, their problems may not be primarily one of ethnic origin. What appears to be an issue of ethnicity or gender might in reality be an issue of social class, and an emphasis on monitoring race does not in itself mean that racial differences are always a 'problem' to be addressed.

> ... treating different aspects of inequality as totally
> separate from one another can significantly distort

analysis and subsequent recommendations. In some cases it can even produce new forms of elitism, that are then institutionalised and legitimised, paradoxically, through discourses of equal opportunities.

Collinson (2006) p14

Regulation 3 requires that colleges:

publish information to demonstrate compliance with the general equality duty (annually)

publish equality objectives (at least every four years).

There must be at least one, it/they must be specific and measurable and ought to focus on the greatest challenge you have identified (no easy targets). They can be short, medium or long term but must reflect and be shaped by consultation with the community (local organisations, networks, unions, partners etc.). You should show how progress will be measured. And it ought to go without saying that when publishing allow for lack of access to IT, disabilities when using IT etc.

So what counts as reasonable behaviour in this context?

If you discipline an employee for out-of-character behaviour but this is caused by medication for a disability then it could be an act of discrimination. It is not enough to show you did not know an employee had a disability. You must show that your environment is sufficiently supportive to allow them to disclose it.

In the case of Pickett v Carpet Express (2002) ET/1400134/02, pinning a notice to the wall to tell employees not to make racist remarks does not amount to a serious attempt to change the culture of the workplace. If the policy is not embedded then it is legally 'inactive'.[27]

It is permitted, indeed encouraged, for educational institutions to discuss differences between groups. What would be illegal would be using a tone of voice or other signal that indicated one group is inferior (= to discriminate or encourage

---

[27] see AOC guide Jan 2012

harassment). Tone of voice might also count heavily when discussing employee rights in public (= at work).

It is illegal to discriminate against men to reduce discrimination against women (e.g. with a quota) but it is perfectly reasonable to encourage more women to apply for a job by advertising in publications and locations and through networks with a high % female readership or membership. You cannot then favour those who seem to be female, judging from clues in their cvs. However, if all other elements are equal and the only difference is that one applicant is from an under-represented group, you may legally favour that candidate, using S.159.

Suppose many popular 14-19 vocational qualifications had their currency reduced. Suppose Engineering came down from four to one GCSE equivalence. At the same time, suppose all public exams required 5% for spelling and punctuation, so that dyslexic students gain fewer marks. Is that reasonable?

You are a manager within education and not a lawyer. It is not your job to answer such questions in terms of legal precedent or likely outcomes in any prosecution. Most providers have experts for that purpose to back you up and bpfe.org.uk/links refers you to plenty of case studies and sources of specialist advice. All you need to do in general terms is to understand what constitutes a civilised society and make sure your area behaves in a civilised manner. In other words, to educate people. To led the way in setting standards.

Is education about skills or behaviour? Which comes first and which is hardest to alter?

> You go to a great school not so much for knowledge as
> for arts and habits.
> For the habit of attention and the art of expression
> For the art of entering quickly into another person's
> thoughts
> For the art of indicating assent or dissent in graduated
> terms

For the art or working out what is possible in a given
time
For taste, for discrimination, for mental courage and
mental soberness
William Cory (1823-93)
lyric poet and master at Eton

The CBI (May 2010) confirmed that:

Employers see it as a priority for the government to
ensure young people develop employability skills to
help make their move into work as smooth as possible.
Thirty-five percent see this as the single most important
action for the government (p13) ... Over half of
employers (56%) believe the biggest single contribution
they can make to preparing young people for entry to a
challenging labour market is to give them opportunities
to gain work experience (p26)

because:

Young people are leaving school and college with
serious weaknesses in their employability. Over half of
employers (57%) are finding weaknesses in school
leavers' self-management skills – such as time
management – and two thirds (68%) believe they have
inadequate business and customer awareness. A quarter
of employers (24%) are dissatisfied with graduates'
problem-solving skills, and 26% with their self-
management skills. (p22)

Among reasons for hard-to-fill vacancies (table 4.10) are
"applicants have not got required attitude". Although
employers often insist that educational failures are causing a
lack of employable skills, what they often mean is that they
can't find employable attitudes. A manager's job is to foster the
right environment.
Another term often misunderstood is "disability".

Disabilities may be medical or social. That is to say, the problem may be caused by an accident of fate or the attitudes of others. It is not just that educational establishments have to lead by example in refraining from bad practice. They have to help forge a civilised and equitable society by shaping behaviour and attitudes, leading the way for the local community. That means several things:

Knowing from local data which sections of the community are under – represented

Knowing which local or national agencies can best advise on the removal of barriers.

Knowing what kinds of policy and staff training will be required to shape institutional behaviour/responses

This can be an apparently minor act:

Admissions staff at one college changed a question on their enrolment form to focus on support options and benefits. They also included prompts in interview guidelines to ensure that staff tell all applicants what support was available for learners with disabilities and learning difficulties. Disclosure rates increased by 30% as a result.   LSDA briefing sheet ref 052015 (2005)

By now, there should also be an increasing awareness within the organisation of just what 'disability' means. It may be obvious or hidden, declared of undeclared. It might, for example, be:

physical, but not necessarily obvious

sensory (deafness or blindness to varying degrees),

dyslexia, or a learning difficulty that is not commonly known to many staff

or a mental health difficulty.

The latter is particularly difficult for non-specialist staff to respond to, and disclosure is less likely if the front-line process is public and intimidating. The key is that it has a "long term, substantial, adverse effect on normal day-to-day activities".

So inequalities exist, and certain areas will still need to overcome significant barriers to ensure equality of access to HE and the job market. Also, the issues implied by those figures are complex and intertwined. If English is a second language for some of FE's potential recruits, will equality of access be improved by ESOL support alone or will racism and religion combine to complicate the picture? The simplest duty of a manager is to know the facts upon which more complex issues may be settled, but even that matter is sometimes over-simplified.

Focusing on evidence not just figures

College A knew from the census that x% of the local population were of BME origin. They knew the percentage of BME students in college was considerably less overall, especially full-time 16-19. But how should they define the problem? A closer look at the figures confirmed three significant facts.

1) With two universities in the area, and a strong tendency for graduates to remain in the area when seeking employment, many of those BME figures were already successes of the educational system, not in need of their assistance. Some of the BME students within the local GFE were post-graduates on short courses to supplement degrees when looking for work.

2) When the measures looked only at students graduating from local secondary schools post-16 - i.e. those who might reasonably be expected to move to FE full-time - it was clear that students from certain groups were still under-represented. However, there were two sixth form colleges in the area and

some schools also had sixth forms. How many BME students had gone to do A levels elsewhere and did not need college A? Were certain groups more likely to be high achievers and thus more likely to be in sixth form colleges than in GFEs? Given that certain BME groups seemed to achieve higher pass rates that the norm within the college, that theory seemed promising, although it begged certain questions of causality. Certainly, it was now obvious that it would not be possible to monitor the GFE provision without knowing application, conversion and success rates in the competing forms of provision which, surprisingly, had not previously been considered.

3) Once they were taken into account, it was possible to see which groups were unreasonably under-represented and whether there were particular differences within vocational areas. However, the groups most under-represented lived in certain post-codes where white British males were also poorly represented in the same ways – the problem seemed to be socio-economic in origin.

This did not mean there were not occasionally issues of racism that might need handling in general terms, or that materials and canteen food and facilities were not in need of adjustment to reflect a more diverse society. It did mean that the greatest barriers to participation were not in themselves caused by factors that were primarily a matter of race, religion or ethnicity from the college's point of view.

It used to be generally assumed that 'young black males' tend to achieve less well than other students. Did that discourage staff from enrolling young black males, or encourage a subconscious tendency to have lower expectations that lead to self-fulfilling prophecies? Does careless use of undigested statistical information just make the matter worse? By early 2007 is was being argued that children from minority ethnic groups tended to progress more quickly than white pupils between key stages 2 and 4, with indications that parental pressure to improve was at least partly responsible. Colleges with out-of-date information will also have out-of-date priorities and expectations.

There was a tendency to talk about suitable role models:

> There are a high number of learners from minority groups in the learning and skills sector. For providers, there are challenges in engaging those learners and keeping them on track and this is exacerbated by issues such as institutional discrimination. An organisational culture which encourages diversity and provides culturally relevant role models creates a more representative learning environment, and leads to better results.   Persaud (2005) p5

The argument may hold in general terms, but there is no evidence that, for example, black male teachers get better results from under-performing black male students. Certainly, HRM need to monitor the ethnic composition of the staff and compare it to that of the students and the local population. They do not need to leap to over-simplified conclusions about cause and effect. Nor should a focus on phrases like BME allow anyone to assume that racism or inequality is always a matter of colour. White refugees and asylum seekers from Eastern Europe, Irish or other travellers are all subject to discrimination. Staff in areas where a mixed community is a relatively recent experience may need guidance on appropriate terminology – who is 'black' and when is it best to speak of 'visible minority ethnic communities'?

Interesting data on discrimination at work, including 'self-reported prejudice' may be found in Heath and Cheung (2006), for example a key finding that

> Overall a number of ethnic minority groups, notably Pakistani, Bangladeshi, Black Caribbean and Black African men continue to experience higher unemployment rates, greater concentrations in routine

and semi-routine work and lower hourly earnings than do members of the comparison group of British and other whites. Women from these groups also have higher unemployment rates than the comparison group although, for those in work, average hourly earnings tend to be as high or higher than those of white women.

As with all forms of inequality, the world of the provider is expected both to reflect the community it serves but also to maintain a much higher standard of behaviour than is normal in that community, despite the fact that the provider, being a microcosm, probably has greater variety in a smaller area and with more close contact than the wider community.

Age, of course, is an issue for employment (retirement age and prejudice in interviews) and for access (fee structure and the overwhelming focus on youth in many reception areas). Religion is another difficult issue to define in general terms. How many colleges finish on Friday in time for Orthodox Jews to be home by the start of Sabbath? Does the rise of a fundamentalist Christian element to some Academies affect application rates from Muslim students? [28]. Are tutors in ESOL courses justified in complaining that some of their female students are not permitted certain freedoms that they hold to be fundamental and have relied on when arranging conversation classes? Where does freedom of expression end and propaganda begin, especially when managing a student's right to post fliers and organise clubs? An example was given in

---

[28] Emmanuel College in Gateshead, sponsored by the Vardy Foundation, is led by an evangelist (TES July 23, 2004 p3). Note also TES March 18th 2005. p6, on the bid for schools by Exclusive Brethren through Focus Learning Trust. FE Focus 13th Jan 2003 Bill Rammel suggested a chaplain in every college would help students explore their spirituality. Complaints about American evangelists supporting Israel in Gaza encourage references to Crusaders among radical Islamic movements. Being even-handed is not an easy, soft option during the occupation of Iraq/post 9-11/ invasion of Gaza (*delete as preferred)

Teaching in FE where the free expression of religious sentiment as part of an oral exam was held to be grounds for failing the exam.

And what about gender?

> Managers supposedly behave in particular, well-rehearsed ways; they are purposeful, rational, decisive, and technologically competent – the subtext here being that change is safe in their hands. Women managers are especially vulnerable to criticism when such stereotypical expectations are not met.
>
> Walker and Ryan, p149 of Ashcroft and James ed.

> Males see their own and their line manager's leadership style as transactional more often than females, who are more likely to practice transformational leadership.... Males were more likely than females to describe both their own and their line manager's activities as transactional, while females were more likely to engage in transformational leadership activities. Females rated the effectiveness of both transactional and distributed leadership higher than males.
>
> Lumby et al pp 24&28

> Feminist studies demonstrate that notions of leadership are often saturated with the gendered, masculine imagery of the assertive, heroic and individualistic male (Sinclair, 1998). Some writers on gender see distancing oneself from the consequences of one's actions as a routine way that men reproduce 'hegemonic masculinity' (Connell 2005). By contrast, feminine leadership styles may be more 'relational' and proximate, based on more personal forms of communication and thus designed to reduce distance between leaders and led (Fletcher 2001).
>
> Collinson (2006)

Does this mean that there are certain traits in female managers that are more likely to produce leadership styles appropriate to FE? If so, it does not mean that male managers cannot also provide such leadership, but it might mean that certain inappropriate 'masculine' qualities are so valued by the majority that female managers tend to overcompensate to maintain what they think of as control? Whilst on the one hand it is argued that women can equal men in most professions as equal, it is also sometimes argued that they are better at customer relations in some fields because of differences in social skills.

In theory, that is not a necessary question. If we know what we want from our managers/leaders then we want it and know how to encourage it from all of them, regardless of gender, and can appoint accordingly. But it does indicate a set of questions to be asked during SAR about any differences in vocational cultures that affect how we treat our staff and students. Are certain forms of self-expression or self-realisation more or less encouraged? Should SAR processes occasionally mix departments and thus alter gender balances to encourage different perspectives?

It is no news that there are gender imbalances in certain vocational areas. It is possible that certain industries would solve their skills shortage and even improve their customer relations by addressing that imbalance. A provider cannot be held accountable for prejudicial working practices within an industry, but it can be accountable for two related problems.

If a work placement is arranged within one of those industries, then the standards of behaviour expected will be those of the provider not those of the industry. This attempt to raise standards might be said to reduce the offers of work placements or apprenticeships. Life is hard enough for a jobbing builder without having to behave differently in the presence of an impressionable young adult. But what seems reasonable on site can sound less so during a formal enquiry with parents and Student Support in attendance.

It may be relatively easy to get more females into

engineering or carpentry and brickwork at the age of 14, thus helping to overcome gender-limitations on career choice. But if the rise on apprenticeship opportunities is not matched when the link course is over, the ladder created by the provider has missing rungs and held out false hope. A success one year becomes a failure two years later. There are external agencies that can advise and assist here[29] but one question to be asked of any data is how far the provider is bringing about real improvements long-term and how far they are only decorating their SAR with short-term claims. The new role of FE as a champion of equal opportunities asks not only that is gets its own house in order, but also that it exports higher standards to all its partners and clients. That is a tough requirement.

Understandably, sometimes, staff may feel overwhelmed by the effects of so many potential problems, and especially by local socio-economic deprivation, as embodied in needy or difficult students they have been trying to help. A wider focus on the whole picture, especially on trends and causes, may help to put their personal efforts in context. Many staff in FE have entered it because they care about the community they serve, but some may be focused on single issues such as gender, ethnicity or disability. They may think creatively only in those areas. Suppose, during an SAR day, you offered a selection of data and the following charts:

social difficulties (area)	college responses	potential improvement

In terms of individuals with particular disadvantages:

---

[29] See bpfe.org.uk/links

personal disadvantages	college responses	potential improvement

In both contexts, problems can be increased by institutional weaknesses:

weakness to avoid	usual ways to avoid it	potential improvements

Reflecting on the potential for distributive leadership, to what extent would that inform a college-wide response and encourage creative work related to local socio-economic inequities?

Adam Smith argued that the greatest tragedy of the poor was the poverty of their aspirations. Socio-economic deprivation tends to limit career choices and one of the ways that FE can benefit from closer contact with employers is to use them to show 14-16 years olds that there is more to national economic life than the four or five jobs they have heard of through their cousins. That is where we can start in the next chapter.

Chapter 7

Engaging with Employers

Leaders therefore need to focus more on the usefulness of qualifications to learners and not on the quantity of qualifications achieved. Even in the good and outstanding colleges, senior managers and governors have prioritised the achievement of individual qualifications as an indicator of success. There has been insufficient attention paid to how well these qualifications help learners achieve their career and employment goals. This is not surprising: the incentives largely ignore the progress made by learners and the value that post-16 provision adds.

Oftsed Sector Report (2011/12) (4)

As a justly-admired FE college principal remarked to a member of the Review panel: "English FE is unique internationally because it works on a deficit model. We compensate for schools that won't educate children to read and write or prepare them for employment, and for employers who won't recruit and train".

Lingfield (2012) 4.7

(Ignorance is) the appointed lot of all born to poverty and the drudgeries of life...the only opiate capable of infusing that sensibility which can enable them to endure the miseries of the one and the fatigues of the other.....a cordial, administered by the gracious hand of providence, of which they ought never to be deprived by an ill-judged and improper education.

Soame Jenyns 1757
Free Enquiry into the Nature and Origin of Evil

Teaching and training will be inspiring, based on

imaginative resources and led by subject and sectoral experts who are also skilled teachers or trainers. More and more learners will be following programmes delivered by providers that specialise in that subject area.   DfES (2006) 1.13

Employer engagement needs to be developed and understood in a more rounded fashion. It is about involving employers in the wider work of a college, and in the development and delivery of provision in ways that are mutually beneficial and suitable for the specific employer and the provider. There is no 'one-size' template which can fit all employers or providers, and nor should there be.   McCleod and Hughes (2005) p4

It is very odd to be arguing that the most vocationally-orientated sector of the education business should have to 'get in touch' with employers, as if it has been living on some other planet for a few generations and not training apprentices throughout its history. And yet is has been a constant refrain for many years. What kind of a problem is this?

There are different levels at which one may approach the question. The lowest level is when a single class tutor approaches employers to gain work experience for their students, sometimes keeping their contact list close to their chest to avoid 'poaching' by colleagues in other areas. The higher levels include re-drafting the entire shape of 14-19 education by asking employers to design the new diplomas, then planning your offer both locally and internationally in conjunction with commercial and industrial partners. If the two levels are not connected so that joined up thinking creates an effective institutional policy then time and opportunities will be wasted and the provider's public image will suffer.

To summarise very briefly, employers too often do not think that the services provided by the FE or LLL sectors are good enough for their purpose. It is not a quality product. When they do receive quality, the product tends to come more often from private agencies than from established colleges:

> 7% of employers who used FE colleges during the last
> year were 'not very' or 'not at all' satisfied with
> provision. 82% of employers did not use colleges at all.
> DfES (2006)
> > citing National Employers Skills Survey (2005)

A dissatisfaction rate of 7% may not sound much, and your
marketing dept could make 93% satisfaction sound impressive,
but it doesn't get much better over time:

> The vast majority were satisfied with the service they
> received from FE colleges (85 per cent, similar to the 84
> per cent found in 2007), though satisfaction with FE
> colleges remains lower than found for training delivered
> by universities or other providers.
> UKCES (2010) p152

> perceptions of the work readiness of different sub-
> groups of labour market entrants varied quite
> considerably. In England, Northern Ireland and Wales
> almost three in five recruiting 16 year school leavers
> found them to be well prepared (59per cent, rising to 64
> per cent of those recruiting 17-18 year olds from
> school, 72 per cent of those recruiting from Further
> Education and 82 per cent of those recruiting from
> Higher Education establishments finding them well
> prepared. Establishments who find recruits from
> education to be poorly prepared most commonly
> attribute this to a lack of "experience" (maturity /
> experience of the working world). They also commonly
> cite attitude/motivation. Acquired skills / competencies
> is a third order deficiency. ibid 2.4

It really shouldn't surprise any employer that a new recruit
lacks experience, but you can see that and any future

relationship needs to overcome an inheritance of traditional suspicion:

> a perceived mismatch between the publicly funded education and training available and the needs of employers and the workforce has been a long-standing concern in the UK. Indeed, employers' representative bodies have often been sharply critical of what they see as deficiencies in government-funded provision. For example, David Lennon, former Director General of the British Chambers of Commerce (BCC) said that "there is a gaping chasm between Further Education and local employers" and that colleges are providing inadequate preparation for students moving to the workplace. John Cridland from the Confederation of British Industry (CBI) has expressed similar concerns, and a recent CBI survey showed that twice as many members rated private training providers as good or excellent (76%), compared to FE colleges (38%).
>
> McCoshan and Souto Otero (2003) 1.2

One might object at once that complaints are by no means one-sided. The TUC report, *2020 Vision for Skills* (2006) claimed that 8,377,200 workers have not been trained, while of those who are, only 11.5 per cent receive a nationally recognised qualification. But then, receiving an NVQ isn't always a necessary part of becoming increasingly useful, and to claim imperfections on both sides is no excuse to go to war with a natural ally. Ex-heads of the CBI include Sir Clive Thompson, whose European Home Retail owned Farepak, responsible in 2006 for taking money from poor savers to subsidise incompetent management. Sir Digby Jones became non-exec director iSoft, a firm embroiled in accounting irregularities, and Lord Marshall (1996-8) later chaired BA and Invensys, both of which underperformed. As for the 2008 financial collapse – one can't blame managers in FE for that. Good managers within FE need not be excessively humble when dealing with what E. M. Forster called the world of anger and telegrams. Human failings exist on both sides, but that is beside the point. More importantly, how many faults are endemic or structural?

There are many strands to this debate which need to be separated, even though they are closely related. One element is the traditional complaint from employers that the raw material provided by education to be their work force do not arrive at their doorstep either job ready or work ready. The former means having all the skills necessary to do the particular job in question, to the right standards - often a narrow set of specific skills. The latter means having the right attitude to work, being able to persuade employers that the applicant really belongs in a place of employment, that they understand the pleasures of work and will contribute to the firm's good health - a wide range of transferable skills and attitudes. This is often the more common and most bitter complaint. Colleges, schools and universities are accused of turning out raw material that is insufficiently literate, numerate, mentally flexible or committed to the idea of work in general. employability' is seen as a set of skills, always including and sometimes especially attitudes or qualities such as enthusiasm; the ability to develop effective social and working relationships; the motivation to continue learning; punctuality, commitment and honesty; the ability to be enterprising and interact confidently; team working, common sense.[30]

> This mission is not narrowly about occupationally-specific training. ....It includes fostering an enterprise culture and .... must extend to inculcating the values, attitudes and knowledge that society seeks from its citizens. - DFES (2006) 2.8

The relation of the curriculum to work readiness, of metacognition and study skills to employability skills, is dealt

---

[30] examples in DfES 2006 4.6, 5.22; LSN 2007; QCA 2006

with in detail in *Teaching in FE*, where it is argued that you cannot produce the kind of young applicants required by employers if the teaching style and institutional culture demands passive obedience and requires more listening than talking. But it also argues that industry often does not know what it needs, and expresses what it wants in a language riddled with false assumptions. This strand of the argument may be called the transferable skills strand, and put to one side for the moment, except perhaps to refer to a comment in Leitch's interim report, citing work from the Centre for Research on the Wider Benefits of Learning (Green et al, 2003) to support the claim that an increase in learning among the most socially deprived leads to a more profitable relationship with employment that can help to increase their health and even their levels of racial tolerance (2005, 1.107). But of course, is there are no jobs.....

Another element of the debate concerns the whole purpose of a local provider and their relation to local market conditions. Chapter one raised the problem of supply and demand and the way it is linked with a confusion of social purposes. For example, to encourage the least motivated school students, FE has provided a range of vocational options. For a` while it was boosted by funding from Increased Flexibility (IF) then we all got slightly excited about Vocational Diplomas. But traditionally, many schools will ask for a very narrow range of options, reflecting the narrowness of their students' experience. Hairdressing, catering, car mechanics, plumbers, bricklayers – they ask for what they or their local families know about. Using this narrow range, the provider will then use that interest, however ill-informed, to develop training that in turn develops the social, cognitive and motor skills that may one day make them work-ready.

Or, of course, the provider could argue that (a) there are only four really successful industries in this area so that is all I shall train you for (b) unemployment is so high in this locality you will need to train for something that takes you elsewhere as soon as possible. Neither will be well-received by schools seeking to increase motivation with demand-led planning.

The short term social and education goals of the school would require an endless supply of link courses in traditional subjects. The long term economic and social purpose requires that students who are taken on should be offered useful employment at the end of the course. It is a major political question how far one ought to (or could) control the supply of labour to match either local or national demand. Should you refuse to train architects or nail technicians because you don't need them this year or within a 30 mile radius?

There are no reliable mechanisms to fine tune supply. Market information to that end can be unreliable and we simply don't have the levers to match trainees to vacancies with any finesse. There are plenty of countries that make life easy for the 'leaders' by limiting student choices and directing labour supply by enforced training in what the 'leader' thinks the country needs, but we are not there yet, not quite. But neither can we ignore the problem when managing education. Ladders of progression need to be planned. It is not acceptable, economically or morally, to take someone on at the age of 14 or 16 or 18 and then, when they work hard and pass, tell them the next rung of the ladder is not available, and never was. That is shoddy work and careless of young people's lives. Some sensible application of Labour Market Information (LMI) is required for responsible planning. How is that balance to be kept?

At the micro level, we need to be better informed and more honest with students when advising them. At the age of 14, when they choose a link course or vocational option, how many of them have actually talked to local employers about what sort of work is available locally, what the prospects are and what the employing agencies are looking for? It would seem reasonable for the college, employers, schools and careers services to work together to provide informative visits that explain to students and parents what the labour market is doing and what work in that context actually means. They should not choose plumbing or nursing or 'being a vet' unless they have listened to a plumber, a nurse and a vet. That kind of partnership can be put together at little expense, and would be much more useful than the traditional pattern, a few stalls around the hall from colleges selling their wares to fill courses, a stand from the army and a surfeit of branded plastic bags and bookmarks for bewildered children to take home. It might be argued, though not without controversy, that proper careers advice cannot easily be provided exclusively by someone whose working life has been spent as a teacher or careers adviser. If employers want well-informed recruits they must come and inform them. We can call this the 'seed corn' strand of the argument. It combines with the use of employers to enhance the curriculum (see chapter 5) and is the kind of activity Hughes et al (2004) refer to when they say:

> Using experts from the world of work adds credibility and authenticity to the learning experience and provides examples of what constitutes excellence. (p45)

Assuming, of course, that local employers are of a suitable standard to model excellence.

It can be argued that choices made at 14 or even 16 are not, and perhaps should not be, final commitments to future careers. The young explorers need the right to change their minds and the new diploma structure will need to allow movement between vocational areas by mapping the transferable elements of their units. Indeed, one of the arguments about a modern work force is that few people can expect to remain in the same kind of work all their lives, so we need more transferable skills, It is also argued that we need a more highly skilled workforce in general as the nature of work changes. Employers want more basic or key skills and FE has to provide them. This might be called the skills shortage strand and it has three quite different sub-sections. What is a skill shortage?

71% of respondents defined a skills shortage to be

present when a client asks to be informed whenever candidates with a specific skill become available. 66% defined it to be when a particular type of vacancy is regularly advertised. 58% defined it to be when a vacancy remains unfilled for a considerable amount of time, whilst a further 58% defined it to be when a vacancy appears that cannot be filled by any candidates on their database. When asked how else respondents would define when a skills shortage was occurring, 28% of respondents identified a situation that involved a client requiring candidates with specific experience rather than a formal or academic qualification.

Watt (2004)

There is another way to define skills shortage, and that is to compare the UK with other countries and ask if we have the same percentage of skilled workers across the population, but for local planning it is more likely to be this kind of local accounting that holds sway. The National Skills Task Force (NSTF) uses three categories. External recruitment problems include **hard to fill vacancies** (htfvs) and **skill shortage vacancies** (ssvs). The latter occur when there are not enough suitably qualified applicants for the former. Internal problems include **skill gaps,** which occur when some existing staff cannot perform a task required by the employer. The number of reported htfvs is increasing and ssvs may occur because of problems with interpersonal and/or generic skills. The National Employers Skills Survey (2005) reported htfvs at 7%, although skills gaps were closing. By 2009 the updated report claimed:

> The proportion of employers with any staff at their establishment not fully proficient at their jobs (i.e. experiencing skills gaps) fell in the period 2003 to 2007 (from 22 per cent to 15 per cent) but has risen for the first time in the series, to 19 per cent in 2009. The proportion of the workforce lacking full proficiency has remained relatively consistent (seven per cent in 2009,

close to the six per cent reported in both 2005 and 2007). Skills gaps are more common in 'lower level' occupations both in absolute terms and in terms of the proportion of those occupations lacking proficiency – nine per cent of elementary staff and 10 per cent of sales and customer service staff are described by their employers as lacking proficiency. By contrast, just six per cent of managers and professionals have skills gaps (p2)

On the basis of such information, what should providers do? If they increase the numbers they train until all the local vacancies are filled with 100% efficient people, would they then have to close the courses again, lay off all the experienced staff and mothball equipment until the next shortage arises? If we are talking of the old models of provision, perhaps so. That is why the old models are not surviving. If, on the other hand, a provider could go to the schools and colleges and Job Centres to drum up interested applicants, then work with the firms in question to train on their premises, a more flexible and sustainable model would evolve. Should they sign on experienced Polish drivers and teach them ESL or give local teenagers first option to mop up NEET figures? Perhaps they could give each experienced Pole a teenage local as an apprentice? Something imaginative is required to offer a flexible solution, and it is likely to differ in each region.

Part of the model would have to involve employers paying for the tailored service and expecting a fee for the provision of staff to solve their problems – a proper commercial trade off. Reduced income from LSC sources will assume that trend.

> The long term aim for employers and learners to contribute more to the cost of their training will require colleges to be more commercially astute.
>
> CPA (2006)

That is the kind of thinking many educational managers are not used to. Because they are not always skilled negotiators, it is common to find colleges appointing business managers to act on their behalf. This is the 'agent for talent' strand of the argument, and it raises several problems. As McCleod and Hughes (2005) point out:

> Increasingly, as specialisation of process or product becomes more common in small firms, learning activities may need to be packaged from a variety of sources, or designed to match the particular context of the company. Solving unique problems requires higher-level (possibly technical) skills and good communications skills. Mentorship and consultancy appear to be highly valued by people managing small firms, but an effective link to the particular context of the individual business appears to be paramount. Two responses to this seem to be required:
>
> developing a greater number of 'specialist' advisers, to match the vast range of circumstances and contexts that may require support
>
> developing the capacity of advisers to relate general principles to specific context and the ability of the receiver of support to put generic principles into context.   - p41

This kind of thinking makes several assumptions:

> That the provider actually has expertise that is up-to-date, high-quality and commercially valuable [31]

---

[31] Example of a college offering expertise to build its own image, and covering the cost – in 2006 East Tyrone College of Further & Higher Education offered seminars to the owners/managers of local SMEs on Time Management, Effective Business Communication, Business Planning, Managing Staff. Sponsored by SMILE project.

That it knows how to deploy it within a commercial environment

That employers would be willing to pay commercial rates for these services, instead of expecting the 'local tech' to act for free as it always did before, albeit without 100% satisfaction.

That the provider can be commercially astute without losing its social role, for which the LSC, a dominant market force, is paying a premium

The first assumption ignores the fact the FE is being reformed precisely because it is said to be out of touch. How can a college sell expertise to employers who think it doesn't have any and turned to the private sector? Universities can sell research because they have something employers don't. What does your institution have that is worth their fees? McCoshan and Souto Otero (2003; 4.3) speak of the need for "college leadership" and "greater inter-departmental cooperation" and argue that funding any form of employer engagement

> constitutes a significant concern for colleges. Current funding arrangements were seen as the most important barrier to engagement, with major concerns around the linking of funding to the achievement of full qualifications and the paucity of resources available to support activities such as up-front marketing to employers. Funding is a particular problem if more colleges are to move towards the provision of the more complex services such as business solutions, research and development and product design discussed in the preceding sub-section, which entail considerable up-front investment of this sort. The proportion of fee income estimated to come from employers was low
> (4.12)

This is hardly a new problem. Chalrton et al, looking at the management of technical colleges in 1971, found that

> Difficulties are being experienced in colleges in maintaining close ties with industry, business and the professional schools. The pressure of internal work … sometimes results in only token efforts to promote liaison. This burden might be reduced by better allocation of time, but it also depends on an increased awareness on the part of Local Education Authorities of the need for more ancillary, clerical and administrative staff in the college (p154)

They found managers spending too much time on routine management tasks and unable to delegate because of the management structure (p46-47). In the early 21st century, with managers cut loose from LEAs and able to do as they please so long as they meet their funder's targets, it was still sometimes difficult, when speaking with staff from traditional colleges, to prise them away from discussions about traditional qualifications, as if funding through the LSC for a full 'qual aim' for a traditional course were the only way they could earn income. In theory, they had the freedom to offer whatever the market wants to charge whatever the market will bear. If they could make income outside the LSC contract through consultancy or on-the-job training, with or without traditional qualifications, there was no reason they should not do so. Except, of course, that they could not imagine what that was like, because they were constrained by experience. Also, they were afraid of acting independently because the dominant client was so large it 'owned' the provider, and the LSC had its own priorities which were not always commercial.

Moreover, managers appointed to improve relations with business sometimes find themselves acting more like mere salesmen, trying to push college services onto local clients, or at best poorly trained 'marketing' people, trying to find what the clients want so it can be repackaged and sold to them. A position advertised in 2006 asked for

> a committed, enthusiastic and dedicated Sales Team Leader to lead and manage the College sales operation, generating exacting income targets and increasing the penetration rate within relevant sectors...

These functions are both necessary, but are not the same as

> working with employers to plan provision long term and monitor trends short-term

> working within the college so that training and working habits within each dept. are linked to market trends, current best practice and ladders of opportunity.

Nor do we always think clearly about what we mean by 'employers'. The SSCs will be dominated by medium to large firms. Local SMEs and sole traders are less likely to have time to spare to join committees. The results of most formal planning will tend to favour the needs of larger firms, when local opportunities may be among the smaller firms. Train to Gain contracts can become a significant feature of the funding stream but this involves working with unions as well as employers.

> Unions have a growing role in promoting training in the workplace. There are now over 12,000 trained ULRs, who play an important role in giving employees the information and confidence to access training.

> DFES (2006) 3.28

It is in this context we need to recall the function of boundary spanners (from Chapter 1). Managers in education need to know their own business – which few others will understand – but also be intimately well-informed of the needs of at least one and often several vocational sectors. They need to have partners at several levels with whom they can work both formally and informally. Relating to 'an employer' may mean knowing the needs of several people within the company, whose views and perspectives are quite different, and may not even be compatible.

This kind of networking is not a traditional function of management in FE, or even some LLL areas, and senior management are not always able to organise middle or line managers without restrictive notions of how their time ought to be used. The old conveyor belt mentality of churning out products from classrooms and workshops by contact hours with qual aims has crept up the ladder to infest people who ought to be imagining a new future. Part of the CPD for a manager in education is to get out more. McCoshan and Souto Otero found that:

> Whilst almost all colleges offer a "common core" of flexible provision such as training outside office hours, less than 50% offer more complex provision such as business solutions, research and development and product design. Such provision requires greater commitment from colleges to be more proactive, to adopt a holistic approach to employer needs and to have higher skills levels amongst their staff.

> Employers' input into curriculum design was most commonly organised at departmental level.... Just over a quarter of colleges also had college wide mechanisms for employer input in this area, and a quarter had mechanisms at sub-departmental level.

but

> The evidence for collaboration between departments is not strong and the lack of integrated approaches to employer contact means colleges risk not knowing who last contacted an employer, why and with what result
> (p17).

Is the problem in your area less with talking to employers than with talking to each other, less with skills among students than with skills among staff?

The Foster Report was clear about the skills FE lacked, and recommended two schemes to solve the problem. *Business Talent* is a management recruitment programme to help colleges and providers attract exceptional talent from business and the public sector into senior management roles. *Business Interchange* will offer FE and LLL staff experience and training in relevant vocational sectors and encourage 'industry experts' to give time to local colleges and providers. On the one hand, government is asking FE to sell its expertise to industry for profit. On the other, it is suggesting it has so little expertise that we need to recruit 50 managers from outside education and 50 graduates every year to add more professional managerial skills.

Meanwhile,

> National Skills Academies (NSAs) can play a leading role in driving these networks. Proposals for NSAs will be led by employers, who will be sponsors, with the support of SSCs. NSAs will deliver high quality training by establishing national centres of excellence in skills and training for the major sectors of the economy. .... They will provide a hub for the development and delivery of high quality vocational and occupational learning in their specialism. They will have a leading role in sharing the latest industry best practice in training design and identifying relevant qualifications. DFES 2006

With NSAs and Learning Brokers and Uncle Tom Cobley developing the power of the contract, it may be hard to know who will have the greatest influence in any future planning period. Boundary spanners need to be able to monitor them, which means facing outwards. It means being able to persuade employers on a page of A4 that speaking to you is worth their while, that you can increase their profits and won't waste their time with a lot of meetings, telephone polls and questionnaires that are focused only on your profits or, worse, still, some purely internal goal.

Finally, of course, some considerable thought needs to be given to the growth of HE in FE. Government policy is very clear.

> In line with the wider mission, there should be a presumption that HE delivered in FE should have a strong occupational and employment purpose. The major area of expansion will be Foundation Degrees. We will also expand work-based HE programmes. ....we set out major new proposals for FE colleges and training providers to play an important part in that, working within the Train to Gain framework to offer integrated training programmes for, and co-financed with, employers, ranging from basic skills to HE.

> DfES (2006) 2.40

The face of HE is changing and in due course there ought to be a ladder from vocational Diploma to, perhaps, a modularised vocational degree system so that modern apprentices can become modern graduates, perhaps without leaving work for three years and amassing debts. Not everyone in HE greets that movement with unalloyed pleasure. Professor Patrick Ainley of Greenwich University used his inaugural lecture to explore the purpose of HE, arguing that, in the "new market state" we have moved from guardians of knowledge to servants of the global corporations. The education system has been tiered – a division of academic and vocational that harks back to the 1950s – but the new social division is between the employed and a new form of underclass.

Whilst employers and government agencies talk of a need to upskill the workforce, Ainley explains that the inflation of paper qualification and the way the economy is managed combine to create a new class of 'under-qualified' who are not wanted by any employer, and are unlikely to be in the foreseeable future. An increasing proportion of the population have qualifications that are not necessary to do their job, creating an oversupply, whilst others are formally excluded from the possibility of work. Engaging with employers will not help this underclass, although FE will almost certainly be held accountable for providing them with 'skills' to improve the NEET figures.

Ainley argues that the effect of the vocational focus in HE has been to turn teaching into telling. Under an illusion of independence, HE deals in a form of generalised knowledge that is

> incapable of questioning the purposes to which it is put or the society that produces it - Ainley (2005) p7

The original polytechnic model was not meant to be narrowly vocational but "aspired to derive generalised knowledge of nature and society from practical application". It had "knowledge for a social purpose". Present reforms do not sufficiently challenge the idea of an elite HE.

Meanwhile, the labour market suffers an increasing division into core workers, who need education and training to cope with a changing market, and a disposable remainder who may be sub-contracted, casual, peripheral and de-skilled. Workers need to be multi-skilled and the jobs that used to be available for unskilled workers now require an increasing level of NVQs. Progression, however, may be horizontal rather than vertical, picking up new skills and/or qualifications to stay on the same level of employment. There are two levels of learning – one educated to comprehend and control the process as a whole (HE) and one receiving the competence necessary to carry out the job.

If one accepts Ainley's argument, then FE has an interesting moral dilemma. To survive at all, it has to change. Many elements of its future shape will be enforced from outside, with commercial pressures taking away business if it does not respond to challenges. Theoretically independent yet constrained by government policies that expect it also to act as a social agent, it is criticised for being too disparate and unfocused even as it is asked to take on new roles. The proper relationship between HE, FE and employers is a question not just of budgets but of the final purpose of education. Are there several purposes, depending of whose education we are speaking? Should there be? Managers in education need a strong, clear view on that question. Governments come and go, initiatives wax and wane. Is there, in your own mind, a central purpose for the activity which underpins any temporary or local pressure? That may be the only compass suitable for the next few years. Or, to put it another way, what is FE, and what is a manager for? The answer to that has to be personal as well as institutional. The function of this text has been to assist a personal journey with institutional consequences.

Good luck.

And if you need any further support just call in to www.bpfe.org.uk.

Annexe 1

Examples taken from FE colleges which you can use when checking your own use of language (and what you really mean by it)

put in place	An activity for managers who have never heard on the words 'implement' or 'establish'. Just because you are a manager now you don't have to stop speaking English.
going forward	Something done by people who have never heard the words "in the future". We never used to say it, so why did we start? Are you listening to yourself?
training	(a) Don't change it, explain it. or (b) I need to prove you have all been on this course to show I have done my job.
breakfast meeting	Explain it before they're awake enough to disagree (and it makes them feel really important).
workshop	This training course is unprepared so just talk amongst yourselves. Alexi Sayle used to claim that "anybody who uses the work 'workshop' who's not connected with light engineering is a twat", which may be a bit extreme, but it comes from a good place.
PowerPoint	A way to impose powerful special effects on information that would otherwise have no point.
total quality control	Measuring everything that can be easily measured, except the interest level of the audience and the final effect.
empowerment	A method of cutting costs whilst imposing additional stress (labelled responsibility) on the lower orders.
human resource	A thing with legs to be used, like a chair, to be sat on then disposed of.
pilot/trial	When we find it doesn't work we'll roll it

	out
roll it out	Scheme starts tomorrow across the whole area - materials and details necessary for success to follow sometime thereafter
re-invent the wheel	Something you claim not to want to do just before you start doing it
building capacity	There is nothing here yet
underpinning knowledge	Knowing why there is nothing there yet
ongoing	Still in the minutes so it must be happening somewhere – I wonder where?
consultant	Someone who no longer does the job but is paid a lot more than those who do to state the obvious then conclude it is all their fault

Q: How many reforms does it take to change a light bulb?
A: An enquiry into that problem has been sitting for some time. Here is a large questionnaire to supply your comments to the committee. Deadline tomorrow.
Q: How can I read it when the light bulb hasn't been replaced?
A: Are we really singing from the same hymn sheet?
Q: How many hymns does it take to change a light bulb?
A: There's a report here on the need for chaplains in the FE sector, to increase our tolerance of other beliefs.
Q: I believe I shall replace the light bulb myself - any objections?
A: Have you completed a Needs Analysis, liaised with Health and Safety and noticed what Finance has just done to your remaining budget?

And for good measure:

The lord and I are in a shepherd/sheep situation, and I am in a position of negative need. He prostrates me in a green belt grazing area; he conducts me directionally parallel to non-torrential aqueous liquid. he returns to original satisfaction levels my psychological make-up; he switches me on to a positive behavioural format for maximal prestige of his identity.
It should indeed be said that notwithstanding the fact that I make

ambulatory progress through the umbrageous inter-hill mortality slot, terror-sensations will not be instantiated within me due to para-ethical phenomena. Your pastoral walking aid and quadruped pick-up unit introduce me into a pleasurific mood-state.

You design and produce a nutriment-bearing furniture-type structure in the context of non-co-operative elements; you act out a head-related folk ritual employing vegetable extract; my beverage utensil experiences a volume crisis

It is an ongoing deductable fact that your inter-relational empathetical and non-vengance capabilities will retain me as their target focus for the duration of my non-death period; and I will possess tenant rights in the housing unit of the Lord on a permanently open-ended time basis.

from five Oxford students, *Times Diary* 4th Feb 1981

Annexe 2 – simple rules.

1) Don't read this page until you have finished the book. If you think there are short cuts you are kidding yourself.

2) Get a grip.

3) But in doing so don't choke the life out of your most important resouces. You manage through other people, so it's not about you, it's about them.

4) Get on with it

5) But look at the map before you set off and analyse the data before you decide. Then get on with it.

6) If you think you need help then ask for it before it's too late. Or, on other words, get a grip.

If you only apply 2 and 4 it won't work.

If you don't apply 2 and 4 it won't wotk.

Bibliography

Ainley 2005	*For Free Universities,* Inaugural Lecture by Professor Patrick Ainley Greenwich University 19th January 2005 isbn 1 86166 210 6 published by marketing office Uni of Greenwich but also downloadable from
AOC 2002	*Ensuring Equality of Opportunity* – Quality Information Pack, February 2002, Rosemary Clark
Ali 2004	*Adult Learning Inspectorate* *Annual Report of the Chief Inspector 2003-4*
ALI 2005	*Adult Learning Inspectorate – Annual Report of the Chief Inspector 2004-5*
ALI 2006	*Learner-centred self-assessment* hard copy and cd rom April 2006
Alterio (2004)	*Collaborative Journaling as a professional development tool,* Maxine Alterio, Journal of Further and Higher Education 28/3 August 2004 pp 321 - 332
Ashcroft and James ed (1999)	*The Creative Professional – Learning to Teach 14-19 year olds* ed. Kate Ashcroft and David James, Falmer Press, ISBN 0750 707402 cited components include Chapt 8 *Managing and Being Managed* by Lyn Walker and John Ryan.
Best (2006)	Joel Best *Flavour of the Month – why smart people fall for fads.* Uni of California Press 2006 isbn 0 520 24626 8
BIS (2010)	Independent Review of Fees and Co-Funding in Further Education in England Co-investment in the skills of the future A report to Ministers in the Department for Business, Innovation and Skills July 2010
Bloome and James 2003	*Educational Research in Educational Practice (1)* by Martin Bloomer and David James in Journal of Further and Higher Education Vol 27 no3 August 2003. Note JFHE can be inspected at
CEML 2002	*Management and Leadership Development: building future supply.* Report of the Advisory Group investigating provision in FE colleges, by private providers and organisations. Centre for Excellence in Management and Leadership. isbn 1-903696-09-7
CBI 2010	*Ready to grow: business priorities for education and skills- Education and skills survey 2010* CBI May 2010, ISBN: 978-0-85201-724-1

Charlton et al (1971)	*The Administration of Technical Colleges,* D. Charlton, W Gent, B Scammels, Manchester Uni Press, 1971
Clarke 2004	*Developing the Learning and Skills Sector – the next stage of reform.* Keynote address presented to the LSDA summer conference 15th June 2004
Collinson 2006	*Leader-led relations in context.* Margaret Collinson and Professor David Collinson Working Paper LUMSWP2005-037 downloaded May 2006 from CEL
Common Purpose 2005	*Courage at work; causes and cures of timid management* research report March 2005
Cox and Smith 2004	*From Little Acorns – towards a strategy for spreading good practice within colleges –* Philip Cox and Vikki Smith LSDA 2004 isbn 1 85338 937 4
CPA 2006	*Securing strategic leadership in the learning and skills Sector Twenty–fifth Report of Session 2005–06* House of Commons Committee of Public Accounts HC 602 16 February 2006 HMSO
DCLG 2006	*Improving Opportunity, Strengthening Society One year on – A progress report on the Government's strategy for race equality and community cohesion,* July 2006 Department for Communities and Local Government: London ISBN-10 1 85112 863 8 / 13 978 1 85112 863 1
Desforges 2001	*Integrating conceptions of learning for advancing educational practices* by Charles Desforges - paper presented at the ESRC Teaching and Learning Research Programme, Second Annual Conference - University of Birmingham, November 2001
DFES 2004	Five Year Strategy for Children and Learners DfES July 2004 Cm 6272
DFES 2005	*14-19 Education and Skills –* Feb 2005 Cm 6476, HMSO
DfES 2006	*Further Education: Raising Skills, Improving Life Chances* March 2006, Cm 6768, HMSO 167682 3/06 JW4524
Ecclestone 2002	*Learnng Autonomy in post-16 Education;the politics and practice of formative assessment,* Kathryn Eclestone, Routledge/Falmer 2002 isbn 0-415-247403 or 247411
Green et al 2003	*Education, equity and social cohesion: A distributional model,* Green, Preston and Sabates, Report 7, Centre for Research on the Wider Benefits of Learning, 2003.
Fielding et al 2005	*Factors Influencing the Transfer of Good Practice* Michael Fielding (US), Sara Bragg (US), John Craig

	(D), Ian Cunningham (US), Michael Eraut (US), Sarah Gillinson (D), Matthew Horne (D), Carol Robinson (US) and Jo Thorp (US) University of Sussex & Demos 2005 ISBN 1 84478 393 6
Hallam 2000	*How can we engage practitioners, managers and policy makers with the research process and its outcomes?* By Professor Susan Hallam - Paper presented at the ESRC Teaching and Learning Research Programme, First Annual Conference - University of Leicester, November 2000
Handy 1985	*Understanding Organisations* Charles B Handy Penguin Business Library 3rd edition 1985 isbn 0 14 009110 6
Heath and Cheung (2006)	*Ethnic penalties in the labour market: Employers and discrimination* Department for Work and Pensions Research Report No 341 Corporate Document Services, Professor Anthony Heath and Dr Sin Yi Cheung 2006 ISBN 1 84123 996 8
Hughes et al 2004	*A cut above – customising a curriculum for excellence in skills development* Maria Hughes, Barry Smeaton, Graeme Hall, LSDA 2004 isbn 1 85338 955 2
James ed 2004	*Research in practice: experiences, insights and interventions from the project Transforming learning Cultures in Further Education. Building effective reearch:5* edited David James LSRC 2004 isbn 1 85338 960 9
Jarvie 1972	*Concepts and Society* I.C. Jarvie, Routledge Keagan AND Paul 1972
Keirsey 1998	*Please Understand Me II - Temperament, character, intelligence* David Keirsey Prometheus Nemesis 1998 USA
Layard (2005)	*Happiness-Lessons from a New Science*, chard Layard ,Allen Lane
Lingfield 2012	*Professionalism in Further Education- Final Report of the Independent Review Panel* *Established by the Minister of State for Further Education, Skills and Lifelong Learning* *October 2012.* The Lord Lingfield Kt, MEd DLitt FCGI DL
LLLUK 2005	*National occupational standards for leadership and management in the post-compulsory learning and skills sector* Lifelong Learning UK 2005
LSC 2005	*Learning and Skills – the agenda for change* LSC, August 2005
Lucas 2004 (a)	*Teaching in Further Education – new perspectives for a changing context.* Norman Lucas, Bedford Way Papers, Institute of Education, University of London. isbn 0

	85473 700 6.
LSC 2002	*Trust in the Future, The Report of the Bureaucracy Task Force:* November 2002 Reference MISC/0270/02
LSC 2003	*Circular 03/09. Success for All - Implementation of the framework for quality and success. Arrangements for agreeing three-year development plans and three-year funding, including headline improvement and floor targets.* LSC May 2003
LSC 2004	Learning & Skills Council Strategic Framework to 2004 - Corporate Plan.
LSC 2005	*Priorities for Success – funding for learning and skills 2006 – 2008* LSC Oct 2005
LSN 2007	*Paving the way from keyskills to functional skills 3 Functional Skills and employability. Key skills support programme* LSN 2007, isbn 1 84572 606 5
Lumby et al (2005)	*Leadership, Development and Diversity in the Learning ands Skills Sector,* Jacky Lumby, Alam Harris, Marlene Morrison, Daniel Muijs, Krishan Sood, Derek Glover, Michael Wilson with Ann R.J. Briggs and David Middlewood LSRN isbn 1 84572 103 9
McCleod and Hughes (2005)	*What we know about working with employers - a synthesis of LSDA work on employer engagement.* Deidre Macleod and Maria Hughes, LSDA , ISBN 1 84572 315 5
McCoshan and Souto Otero 2003	A. McCoshan and M.Souto Otero, *Further Education Colleges' Views on FE-Employer Links Andrew McCoshan and Manuel Souto Otero, ECOTEC Research and Consulting Limited,* Research Report RR442, ISBN 1 84478 009 0, June 2003
March 1985	J G March *The Technology of Foolishness* in Organisation Theory 2nd edition edited by D S Pugh 1985 Pelican
Martinez 2001	*College improvement: The voice of teachers and managers* Paul Martinez, Learning and Skills Development Agency 2001 ISBN 1 85338 671 5
Morris and Stanton 2000	<u>*User engagement and research impact in the FE sector*</u> Andrew Morris, and Geoff Stanton. Discussion paper presented at the ESRC Teaching and Learning Research Programme, First Annual Conference - University of Leicester, November 2000
Muijs et al (2006)	Leadership and leadership development in highly effective further education providers. Is there a relationship? Daniel Muijs, Alam Harris, Jacky Lumby, Marlene Morrison and Krishnan Sood in Journal of Further and Higher Education Vol 30 No 1 Feb 2006

	pp87-106 Routledge
NSTF 2000	*Skills for all: Research Report from the National Skills Task Force,*Produced for DEE, 2000
NCSL 2006	National College for School Leadership. Material for the National Professional Qualification in Headship (NPQH)
Ofsted 2004	*Improvement through inspection An evaluation of the impact of Ofsted's work,* Peter Matthews, Pam Sammons, HMI 2244 July 2004
Ofsted (REFE) 2005	*Race Equality in Further Education (FE) – a report into progress and good practice in colleges in the FE sector in response to the Race Relations Amendment Act 2000.* November 2005 HMI 2463
Ofsted TLC 2006	*The logical chain: continuing professional development in effective schools* Ofsted 2006 HMI 2369
Ofsted 2012	*Sector report 2011/12: Learning and skills* Ofsted 2012
Persaud 2005	*Leading Change in Diversity and Equality - The Centre for Excellence in Leadership's Strategy for Improving Diversity in Leadership in the Learning and Skills Sector.* Deborah Persaud March 2005
Postman and Weingartner 1969	*Teaching as a Subversive Activity* Neil Postman and Charles Weingartner USA 1969 page refs to Penguin 1971
QCA 2006	*Report of Consultation on Draft Functional Skills standards;* January to May 2006, Sue Georgious, QCA , June 2006, FSPPB 12 paper 4
Salaman and Thompson 1973	People and Organisations d G. Salaman and K Thompson London Longman for OU,1973
Showers et al 1987	Showers B, Joyce B, Bennet B *Synthesis of research on staff development: a framework for future study and a state-of-the-art analysis.* Educational Leadership, 45 (3), 77-87
Sarason 1996	Seymour B Sarason, *Revisiting "The Culture of the School and the Problem of Change"* New York, Teachers College Press isbn???
Stanton 2000	the chapter by Geoff Stanton on Research in *FE Re-Formed* ed Alan Smithers and P. Robinson, Falmer Press 2000 ISBN 0750709065
Smith 2004a	*A rolling stone gathers no moss maintaining the momentum of action research* John Maynard and Vikki Smith, LSDA ISBN 1 85338 987 0
Smith 2004b	*From Little Acorns : towards a strategy for spreading good practice within colleges* - Vikki Smith and Phil Cox, **LSDA 2004** ISBN 1 85338 937 4
Smith 1973	*Psycholinguistics and Reading,* Frank Smith Holt Rinehart

	and Wilson USA 1973
Smith and Bailey (2006)	*Measuring Cinderella – Measurement 1 – Vital Statistics* Annette Smith and Dr. Andy Bailey, working paper from CEL 2006
Statz and Wright 2004	Cathleen Statz (Rand Corporation) and Susannah Wright (Dept of Eduational Studies, University of Oxford) *Emerging Policy for vocational learning in England. Will it lead to a better system?* LSRC research report 2004
Styles and Fletcher 2006	*Provision for learners aged 14-16 in the FE sector* Brian Styles and Mick Fletcher LSDA 2006 Ref No: 062451
Surowieki 2004	James Surowiecki, The Wisdom of Crowds, 2004, Doubleday isbn 0385 50386 5
TLRB 2005	*Improving Learning in Further Education: a new, cultural approach* *Teaching and Learning* Research briefing no 12, November 2005 referring to the project Transforming Learning Cultures in Further Education (2001 - 2005) run through the Teaching and Learning Resource Programme
UKCES 2010	*National Employer Skills Survey for England 2009: Main report Evidence Report 23* August 2010 UK Commission for Employment and Skills
Wilson 1975	*Educational Theory and the Preparation of Teachers,* John Wilson NFER, 1975
Watt 2004	*Skills Shortages in Somerset,* a research report by Chris Watt of efeedback Ltd, LSC.
Yurchak 2005	Alexei Yurchak *Everything was forever, until it was no more: the last soviet generation.* Princetown December, 2005, isbn 0 691

Teaching in Further Education
Isbn 978-1482730876
Paperback and Kindle on Amazon

Mentoring, training and interim management
www.bpfe.org.uk

web based information on
barriers to learning
www.personalisedlearningforum.eu

3596570R00099

Printed in Great Britain
by Amazon.co.uk, Ltd.,
Marston Gate.